a BRISTOL EYE

For Mum and Dad

Front cover: Colston Street; back cover: All Saints Lane.

Acknowledgments

Many of the photographs in this book exist because so many people responded with enthusiasm and curiosity to my requests for access. I am especially indebted to the Bristol Museums Service and Bristol City Council, to the staff of Bristol University, to All Saints and the Roman Catholic Cathedral. My special thanks go to the people who allowed their homes to be photographed.
Dedicated to my Mum and Dad.
Stephen Morris. Bristol, September 2001.

a BRISTOL EYE

the city seen from new perspectives

Stephen Morris

Tim Mowl

redcliffe

First published in 2001 by Redcliffe Press Ltd.,
81g Pembroke Road, Bristol BS8 3EA
Telephone: 0117 973 7207

Copyright: text Tim Mowl, photographs Stephen Morris (save where assigned to Bristol Museums & Art Galleries)

ISBN 1 900178 78 8
British Cataloguing-in-Publication Data.
A catalogue record for this book is available from the British Library.

All rights reserved. No part of this publication may be reproduced, stored in a retrieval system, or transmitted, in any form or by any means, electronic, mechanical, photocopying, recording or otherwise, without the prior permission of the publishers.

Designed and typeset by Stephen Morris Communications, smc@freeuk.com, Bristol and Liverpool,
and printed by Hackman Printers, Tonypandy, Rhondda.

Bristol – The Undiscovered City

Stephen Morris and I met early in 2000 when he was taking my photograph, looking suitably scholarly, in my study in Cotham for a profile for *The Architects' Journal*. That was to accompany an article publicising the launch of my latest book, *Stylistic Cold Wars – Betjeman versus Pevsner*. Stephen was new to Bristol and keen to learn more about the place so I immodestly put him on to two books I had written in the distant past – *To Build the Second City*, on the city's eighteenth-century development, and *Last Age of the Merchant Princes*, dealing with its Victorian expansion. It was almost ten years since *Merchant Princes* appeared and I had always wanted to bring the story up to date with a book on the failures and successes of the twentieth century. John Sansom of Redcliffe Press had, however, commissioned Tony Aldous to write that study, and so the idea of another book on Bristol had to be shelved.

Then, when I was doing my civic duty, acting as a volunteer guide to the Old Council House one *Open Doors Day*, I saw Stephen in the throng of visitors craning to achieve impossible angles on the sumptuous Greek Revival detail there. What intrigued us both was how so many Bristol interiors were virtually unknown and only ever open on these special days. The idea was formed to search them out and to seek new perspectives on buildings supposedly well known but in reality unremarked. The working title was *A Bristol Detective*, but when it came to the final decision we settled on *A Bristol Eye* to give the impression that this would be visually a new vantage point on both familiar and unfamiliar Bristol buildings. So the book sets out to encourage the reader to discover the city afresh, just as the *I-Spy* books of the 1950s and John Betjeman's TV programmes introduced me to church crawling and the pleasures of architecture.

There are some broad themes running through the text and pictures – interiors, sculpture, dockside, domestic housing, commerce – and the book is intended as an idiosyncratic and frankly often opinionated architectural and historical guide to the city. It is arranged roughly geographically with The Centre at the hub; there are some forays out into the closer suburbs, but the emphasis is firmly on the inner city and Clifton. Go out and see what has excited us and then make you own discoveries; make your own judgements and challenge mine. Bristol has never been consciously planned, like its elegant if rather monotonous neighbour Bath, so there are inducements around every corner and in every conceivable style. Diversity is the key from Quaker classicism through Victorian eclecticism to Art Nouveau, Art Deco and High-Tech functionalism. Bristol has the most poetic eighteenth-century Rococo interior in the country and a decaying nineteenth-century ballroom straight out of Belle Epoque Paris. There is a former riverside police station converted to an elegant restaurant, a Regency Gothic house fit for Keats, a 1970s café that would have delighted the Barcelona architect Gaudi; the surprises are endless. If this book makes you look twice as you pass familiar buildings in your daily round then it will have served its purpose.

Tim Mowl. Bristol September 2001.

Bristol City 2 : London Town 0

Avon Street Bridge

While London was having its public relations disaster in Millennium Year over the much trumpeted 'Wobbly Bridge' across the Thames to Tate Modern, Bristol was quietly, and with quite uncharacteristic brilliance, enjoying two entirely stable yet exhilaratingly daring engineering triumphs over its own more static waters. Everyone knows the Horn or Pero's Bridge, linking Queen and Millennium squares, but this snake-like sinuosity over The Cut, upstream from the Temple Way crossing, has not been given the publicity it deserves. It makes the point that engineering generates its own lively aesthetic whereas the lumpish, loutish buildings which this bridge serves have no aesthetic charm whatsoever, even though they make highly functional offices. The city had a vision of links across waterways, but then the developers lost it.

New Cut Short Cut

Netham Lock, Feeder Road

The New Cut, that ugly muddy ditch that short circuits the Floating Harbour, was completed in 1809, but to link the Kennet and Avon Canal and the Avon Navigation to the Floating Harbour and the sea, the straight Feeder Canal had to be cut from close to Temple Meads station to Netham, with a lock and a trim little lock-keeper's lodge. The lock will take vessels of 24.4 metres length and 5.4 metres beam. Its gates are kept open as long as the water level in the Avon between Netham and Hanham is above the level of the water in the Harbour. Sailors are warned that currents in the Avon can be very strong and they are in danger, as they try to enter the lock from upstream, of being swept down over Netham Weir. As the speed limit in both the Avon and the Feeder is a strict 4 mph it must make boating on this stretch a curious mixture of rest cure and terror.

An Earlier Kind of Edwardian

St Mary Redcliffe, Redcliffe Way

After its north porch the rest of St Mary Redcliffe, Bristol's mini-cathedral, comes as something of an anti-climax. Rich as are its choir and transepts, there is nothing in St Mary's to equal the dazzling unpredictability and spatial enrichments of that octagon with three doors and an inner vestibule in an entirely different style. Architectural historians never like to stress the fact, because of his unfortunate end in the dungeons of Berkeley Castle, but the reign of King Edward II (1307-27) saw English Decorated Gothic at its peak of curvaceous subtlety and artistic invention. That was when Bristol Cathedral's innovative choir was built and when the north porch of St Mary's, with its nodding ogees and unique triple-ogee central door, was projected, possibly as a chapel to house a sacred relic for easy access. There is nothing else in the country quite like it, except perhaps the Lady Chapel of Ely Cathedral. This is what our Gothic could have been if the dreary angularities of Perpendicular had not been forced upon us by the shortage of craftsmen after the Black Death.

Sea-faring Sphere

Redcliffe Quay

When Standard Life Assurance wanted to make a generous gesture to Bristol in 1991 they had chosen a difficult time artistically. Figurative sculpture was temporarily unfashionable and abstracts are rarely popular - so they opted for symbolism. James Blunt's armillary sphere is poised on top of an obelisk of sea monsters and zodiacal beasts composed of densely packed ceramics and fragments of glass. This was designed and created by Kennedy Collings and Phillipa Threlfall and represents 'The Unknown Deep'. The sphere is a device for indicating the movement of the heavenly bodies and is meant to celebrate the daring Bristol navigators who explored the unknown oceans.

Set in a little piazza on Redcliffe Quay the monument livens up that grim line of Hanseatic-looking converted warehouses along Redcliffe Back. Next time could we have bronze seamen battling a storm in a new Bristol Baroque?

5

Victorian Pub Quiz

8 Victoria Street
The late-Victorian façade of what was once a public house on Victoria Street is part of a row of premises that exemplifies the uncertainties and compromises of present-day urban planning. Before the blitz of 1940 such pleasant jumbles of architecture – seventeenth, eighteenth and nineteenth-century – were commonplace in the city, but first the bombs and then grossly misguided post-war planning swept away whole areas of textured cityscape. The Temple precinct was particularly badly hit, a former residential suburb newly zoned for light industry and subsequently shattered in scale by the gargantuan Robinson Building at Bristol Bridge. But, almost by accident, this row survived, unkempt, occasionally used as a tramps' doss house, but human in scale and still defining the bounds of a generally unattractive street with a little charm and variety. The site was valuable. Developers were poised, but by the 1980s aesthetic awareness had grown more generous in its appreciation and the conservationists fought off demolition. Finally a typical compromise was achieved. Most of the row, perhaps three-quarters of it, has been cleaned and restored. But next door to the Courage pub (see if you can guess its name) the last few premises have gone and a bland new brick building has gone up. This takes full commercial advantage of the space and pays merely a token recognition to the storey heights of the older buildings while subtly dwarfing their scale.

A Rock Venue on Water

The Grove

Bristol must always have been the major port in Europe most remote from the sea. When the Saxons abandoned the Roman harbour at Sea Mills and moved even further inland they set up basically insoluble problems for the later Merchant Venturers. But at least we still have the *Thekla* – snub-nosed, flat-bottomed and entirely graceless – an ex-sand dredger like the ship that used, back in the 1950s, to come in regularly once a week to the yard on Redcliffe Back, upsetting all the traffic by raising the bridge on Redcliffe Way. For a time it compromised, coming up to the Hotwells yard. Now the city has given up pretending to smell salt breezes and the *Thekla* is an atmospheric rock venue with acoustics that have to be experienced.

7

Riverstation – the Enchanted Cop-Shop

The Grove

Bristol Harbourside should be wildly picturesque: a natural tourist draw, the Venice of the West with waterways interpenetrating a medieval and classical city. It manifestly is none of these things, and before the planners let any other big schemes through, like those repetitive blocks of gabled flats that keep going up at Wapping Wharf, they could do worse than take an appreciative look at the Riverstation and Merchant's Quay opposite. The Riverstation is a light, airy conversion by Mike Richards of Inscape Architects of the old harbour police building, pleasant by day, transformed by night into tiers of balconied lights, doubled by reflections in the dark water. Thoughtful, underplayed conversions of real harbour buildings work better than phoney, gabled total rebuildings. Merchant's Quay succeeds by playing cautiously with eighteenth-century terrace proportions and by colour contrasts of brick and stucco. With the Thekla and St Mary Redcliffe this is easily the most convincing section of the docks.

Heavy Brickwork, Heavy Metal

The Granary, Welsh Back

As Archibald Ponton and William Venn Gough designed it in 1869 The Granary was the purest Victorian functionalism. Its angles concealed lifts to carry up the grain and then a Heath Robinson system of chutes carried it effortlessly down again to shoot out of those black and white roundels into the carts waiting on the quay. Ten storeys of harsh Cattybrook bricks, relieved by bands of Bath stone, weigh oppressively down on the gallant fragility of polished granite columns in a worryingly underscaled ground floor loggia. Up above Tuscan merlons jag aggressively at the sky. Beautiful it is not; characterful it most certainly is, and was never more appropriately used than when Heavy Metal bands played there in the 1980s to hundreds of leather-clad bikers.

An Ancient Mariner

Cabot on Narrow Quay

This statue of John Cabot, looking pensively out across Bristol's inner harbour towards the open sea, makes the point that all the abstract sculpture on which so much money and argument has been lavished over the last 50 years has been a shocking misdirection of spirit. As photographed here Cabot is dappled with snow patches; a more characteristic shot would have caught the mariner with a small child scrambling over him or sitting in his bronze lap. For this is an art work which has been loved, used and handled from its first inception. Like St Peter's foot in Rome's cathedral, Cabot has been worn golden by fondling.

No one knows what the Genoese Italian Giovanni really looked like, but Stephen Joyce has made a convincing shot at recreation with a mature, middle-aged man, muscular yet elegant in his hands, determined and severe in his lined facial features. His Cabot is not standing to pose noble and artificial on the quayside from which his ship, the *Matthew*, set sail in 1497. Instead he sits pondering how to cope with the Merchant Venturers of Bristol, that closed body of entrepreneurs who have been aware, for at least the last twenty years, that out across the Atlantic towards Iceland there is a patch of sea where cod can be scooped out of the water by the bucket load. It is 'stockfish' – salted cod - that primarily interests the Merchant Venturers, not that harsh shoreline dimly glimpsed through prevailing mists, though at least one merchant, John Jay, had sponsored a ship in 1480 to search for the 'Isle of Brasile'. John Cabot was the real Venturer, the man who could, if only Bristolians had been a little less secretive and possessive about their distant fish larder, have grasped for England the honour that another Genoese Italian, Christopher Columbus, would soon seize for Spain: the discovery of the New World. No wonder Cabot looks angry and has turned his back on the city.

The Language of Cranes

Railway Wharf

Back in the seventeenth century the Great Crane was a famous feature of Bristol's dockside. This Fairbairn steam crane was a nineteenth-century updating from Stothert and Pitt's engineering works in Bath. It was installed in 1876-8, could lift weights of 35 tons (none of the 17 cranes then operating in the harbour could lift more than 3 tons) and was in regular use until 1973. The artist John Piper had a theory that all nautical artefacts like buoys and beacons and navigation lights had a functional beauty of pure form. Would he have been able to fit an arthritic old dowager like this crane into his theory?

A Bus Stop with no Buses @ Bristol

@ Bristol, Canons Road

@ Bristol is a fascinating area, fastidiously detailed and designer-conscious, but will it ever meld convincingly with the rest of the city? This delicate confection of steel and glass by Wilkinson Eyre Architects protects people coming out of the Millennium Square car-park if it happens to be raining. Around it there is a rarefied cluster of shimmering water features and a Brave New World mirror-glass exhibition ball. How will it all weather? How, to quote that *Punch* cartoon mocking the Arts & Crafts movement, shall we live up to it? Lowering heavily over all these exquisite gift-shop novelty items stand the Lloyds buildings like left-over remnants of Imperial Rome. Perhaps the stylistic discord of the place is essentially Bristolian; after all, what has Clifton to do with Corn Street or Broadmead with Kingsdown?

A Secret Garden in a Cathedral Close

College Green

When viewed from College Green, Bristol Cathedral looks exactly what half of it really is: a clumsy Victorian fake. George Edmund Street's nave of 1867-76 and its fourteenth-century choir balance in notably unpicturesque symmetry, one on each side of the central tower, with no relieving break of aisles, side chapels, cloister or ancillary buildings. But here, seen from the south, a satisfying medieval confusion of rooflines and buttresses rises above a small secret garden, accessible only from the cloister. There are graves among the flowering bushes including one to the composer Walford Davies (1869-1941), Master of the King's Musick. To the left, beyond this quiet green plot, is the low gabled roof of the Norman chapter house. Lurching up behind it the awkward stepped roofline reveals where the medieval master mason of that astonishing choir vault had difficulty linking the vaults of the boxy Newton Chapel, built of creamy Dundry stone, with those of the south transept, faced in red Pennant. To their right the Berkeley Chapel with its Decorated tracery disguises the fact that an aisleless hall church, while impressive within, tends to present a gaunt exterior with a cliff of tall windows like those on the cathedral's ugly north face.

Greenery Yallery Café Society

38 College Green

Anyone who can name the building from which this inspired piece of perverse design is dangling must either go around with their head in the clouds or have a keen eye for the Art Nouveau. It hangs from what was the old Cabot Café at 38 College Green, designed in 1904 by the firm of James Henry Latrobe and Weston, who also designed the Whiteladies Picture House. The café was the exact Edwardian contemporary of the astonishingly attenuated tea rooms that Charles Rennie Mackintosh and his wife Margaret Macdonald were designing in Glasgow. But while the Scottish City of European Culture for 1998 devoutly restored and valued its Art Nouveau heritage, so far Bristol shows no interest in a restoration, even though the city is considering a bid for European Culture status in the near future. Bristol never went overboard for the Art Nouveau. It was, apparently, too effete for a sturdy, merchant-dominated west-country city that limited its architectural excesses to the Arts and Crafts movement, a native school of design, and looked with suspicion at anything sinuous, suggestive and Belgian.

The Cabot Café plays a cautious aesthetic game. Its Art Nouveau commitment is constrained to a band of subtly writhing glass mosaic between its first and second floors, flanked by copper hoods embossed with the characteristic lotus blooms of the style. Higher up the decorative detail returns to safe, classically-inspired Beaux Arts. In western afternoon sunshine the mosaic catches the light with almost Byzantine effects. If some councillor with vision is thinking of returning the Cabot Café to its original state as part of the City of Culture bid, its interiors probably still retain their fireplaces with repoussé copper galleons, and there are photographs of its cheerfully exotic first condition.

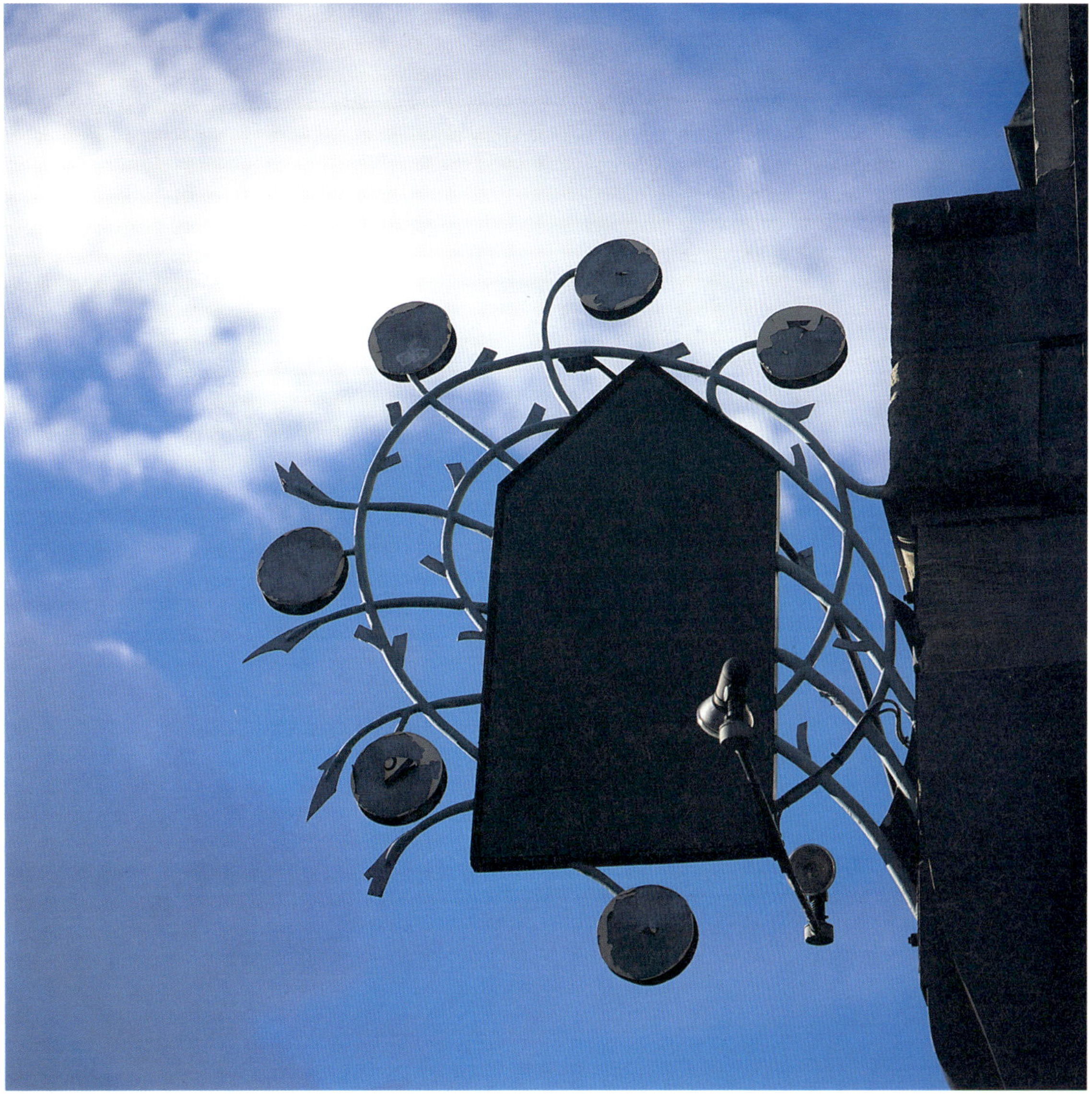

Scandinavian Good Taste Two Decades Late

Council House, College Green

It is probably too early, in a stylistic sense, to pass judgement on the 'new' Bristol Council House as it was designed in 1938, an unfortunate time when the neo-Georgian pomps of the early twentieth-century were giving way to functional modernism. Emanuel Vincent Harris was old-fashioned and unashamed of the fact, so he gave the city a building which would have looked more at home in Edwin Lutyens' New Delhi - big, but full of small details and only just rescued by the two unicorns rampaging on the roof and the heavy pavilions which anchor it down at the sides. If the building had been designed in 1956, the year when it was ceremonially opened, it would probably have been much worse, but that is faint praise. Harris was also responsible for the 1932 County Hall in Taunton, a mini-version of Bristol.

Inside the Council House the detail is a cross between Art Deco and Scandinavian simplicity; that patch of darker red leather on the left of one of the double doors is not part of the design, but the place where thousands of greasy hands have pushed it open. The clock in the entrance lobby, which was designed by the architect and records the zodiacal signs, winds and time, is a nostalgic attempt to prove that Bristol councillors and aldermen were still interested in whether the wind would blow the city's merchant ships up the Bristol Channel on a favourable gust.

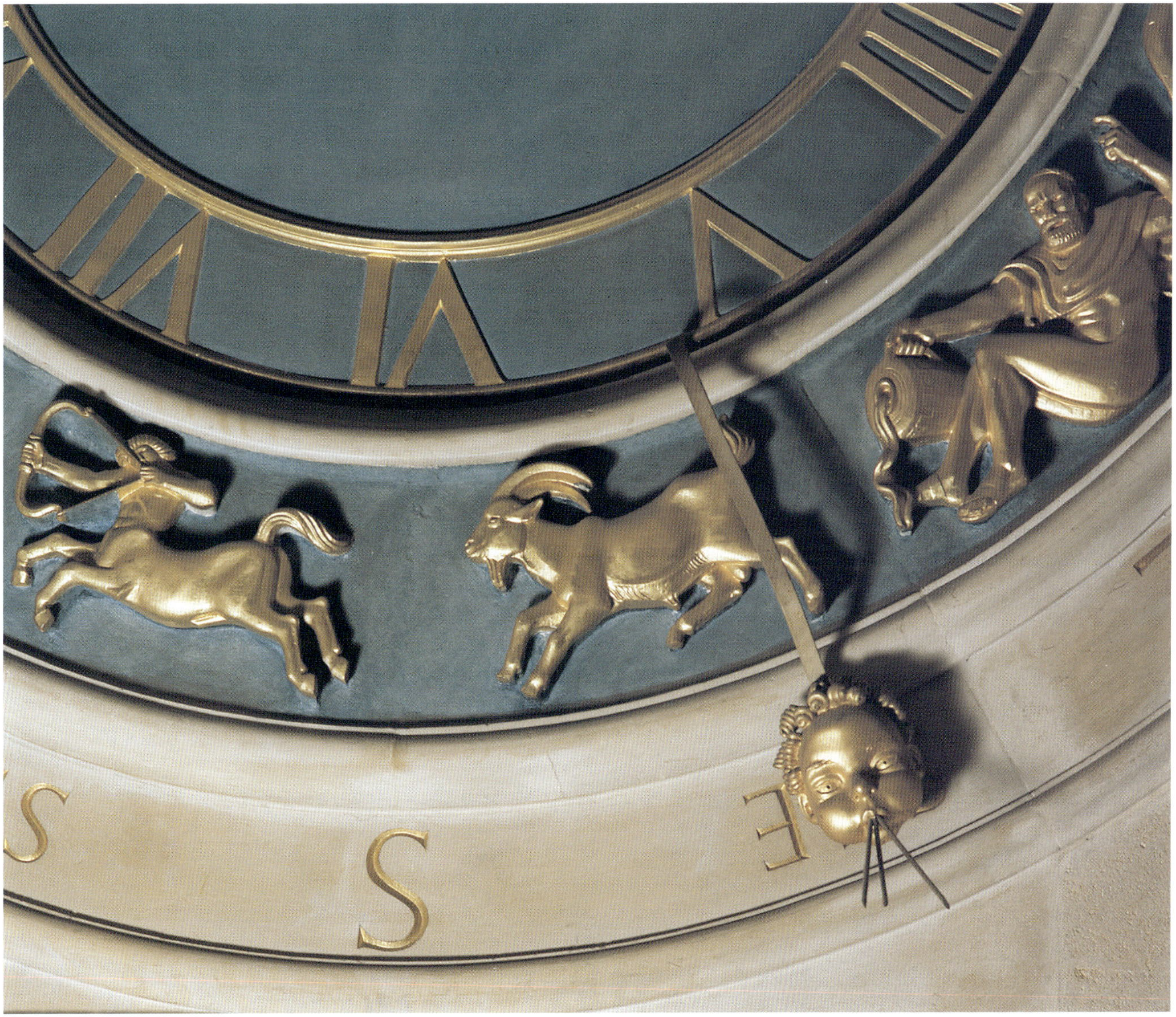

Pylons of Puce and Purple

Fountains at St Augustine's Parade
One local politician described them memorably as the kind of municipal monument you might expect to find in Communist East Germany outside the Stasi Police HQ. But a very capitalist feature about all the latest additions to the Bristol streetscape is that, like these electric pylons in the Centre, they cost money every day to keep them going. Think of the spasmodically squirting fountains at the pylons' feet and those flowing water walls in Millennium Square. What are their day-to-day electricity bills? The trouble with the pylons is that in daytime the solemn row of metal cylinders stepping down to the harbour does something funereal to the civic centre space they occupy. Crematoriums come to mind. Even at night their muted show from puce to purple is down-beat. Are they meant to sober late-night drinkers? Do they symbolise the forward march of a Socialist state? What is their proposed shelf-life?

A Sea God with Hairy Armpits

Neptune at St Augustine's Parade

Neptune clearly should be the city's symbol and its favourite public emblem, a reminder that this completely land-locked place owed all its wealth to the sea. It is, however, hard to get emotional about the sea god's representation in St Augustine's Parade, and from his past history no one seems to have been very keen to have him around for long. He was made in 1723 by Joseph Rendall and first stood on the reservoir of the Temple Conduit in Temple Street. After occupying various sites in Temple, in May 1949 the unpopular god was brought to the Centre and the harbour's edge. He is a very middle-aged Neptune with a bulging stomach and hairy armpits, and while a lead statue can achieve an attractive patina over the years or be treated with paint that looks like sandstone crossed with human flesh, our Neptune has been painted an unimaginative, muddy grey.

Then there is the Animal Rights issue: just what is he doing to that dolphin, holding it out of the water by its tail? Sited as he was on the edge of the harbour, Neptune cut a reasonable profile and related, at second hand, to the sea. Now he just looks bad-tempered and isolated.

Death of a Princess

Sabrina Fountain at Narrow Quay

This bronze fountain by Gerald Laing gains enormously by its siting in a shadowy courtyard behind Broad Quay House, often railed off from the public by iron gates that lend a mystery to the obvious conflict implied in the grouping. Sabrina was a Romano-British princess who drowned herself in the river Sture from grief at the death of her lover Estrildis. The god Nereus transformed her into the patron nymph of the river which was then called after her, the Sabrina or the Severn. Laing, however, has created his own symbolism around the naked lady. The little boys represent adolescents embarrassed by beauty and sexual awareness. Their various poses indicate the immature way young males react to female maturity and confidence.

Bristol's History in Ceramics

Broad Quay House, Narrow Quay

One of the major advances in the new buildings put up in Bristol in the last twenty years has been the incorporation of artwork – free-standing sculptures, lively finials, armillary spheres and sculptural panels. These three mural plaques, which form part of a series of panels by Philippa Threlfall depicting Bristol's history, are just above eye level on Broad Quay House, at the south-east corner of The Centre. The first is based on an eighteenth-century tobacconist's sign showing a 'black boy' (as in Black Boy Hill) against a formalised tobacco plant, a design taken from the WD & HO Wills archive. Next comes a seventeenth-century medal struck by Prince Rupert's Royalist army to celebrate their capture of Bristol from Parliament's forces in 1643. It shows the city as viewed from the south. Lastly, the thirteenth-century common seal of the Burgesses of Bristol shows a ship approaching the watergate of Bristol Castle.

Bristol's Stones of Venice

Lloyds Bank, Corn Street

This glorious defiance of modern good taste and decorative timidity was built as the West of England and South Wales Bank in 1854-8 by William Bruce Gingell and Thomas Royce Lysaght. But the credit for its resounding impact upon the Corn Street scene must go to the sculptor, John Thomas, and, in all fairness, to the sixteenth-century Italian sculptor and architect, Jacopo Sansovino, whose Biblioteca Marciana in Venice was the model for it all. Whereas Gingell and Lysaght invented nothing, simply stealing six bays from Sansovino and dropping them down to outface John Wood's eighteenth-century Exchange across the way, John Thomas did actually exceed his Italian master in the depth and detailed richness of his grotesque keystones, paired female figures of the arts, industries and sciences, and in that riot of industrious small boys hyperactive on its cornice.

What is so challenging about the whole composition is how to rank it in terms of architectural merit. If English copies of original Italian villas like Lord Burlington's at Chiswick and Lord Westmorland's at Mereworth are great architecture, as is generally accepted, how does Lloyd's, Bristol rate? Is it perhaps not architecture at all but an enormous sculpture, three-dimensional where a normal building would be two-dimensional? Sansovino's Biblioteca is almost lost in the complexity of the Piazza San Marco, but Gingell and Lysaght's bank hits Corn Street like some visual armed fist. There is a re-evaluation needed here.

A Baluster for the Wheeler-Dealers

20

Nails at Corn Street

The sausage seller's straw boater rests askew on Master Robert Kitchen's historic brass nail, one of four, outside the Exchange. Before the Exchange was built between 1740 and 1743, Bristol merchants did their business deals in the Tolsey where these nails were set under a loggia. The four balusters were used to pay out money, the coins being rung down on the brass to test if they were sound coinage or fakes; this gave rise to the saying: 'to pay on the nail'. One is sixteenth-century in date, Robert Kitchen's was a gift to the city on his death in September 1594, and the other two date from 1625 and 1631.
The boater is strictly twenty-first century.

Grecian Detail for Bristol Democrats

Council Chamber, Corn Street

When the magisterial *Bristol: an architectural history* was published in 1977, one of its three authors, Andor Gomme, wrote that he admired the spatial handling of the Council Chamber, lit like Wesley's New Room by a lantern, but felt that on its ceiling 'there is a little too much coffering going on'. It is easy to see, from this gloriously rich Greek Revival detail, what he was complaining about, but he was writing in that dreadful Brutalist period when sin and decoration were still believed to be synonymous. This old Council Chamber is in fact one of Bristol's greatest interiors, polychromatic and perfectly in tune with the civic feeling of its period.

Sir Robert Smirke was given the job of designing the new Council House on the strength of his St George's, Brandon Hill of 1821. The Council House was completed in 1823 to a highly critical reception because it takes the corner of Corn Street and Broad Street at a rather indecisive angle. Now that the councillors have left and the lawyers are safely housed in new courtrooms nearby, the room is in desperate need of regeneration. The rumours are that it may well become the city's venue for marriage celebrations. If that were the case brides could dress to accord with the sumptuous Greek decoration in long flowing, high-waisted dresses and wearing seductive dark eyeliner.

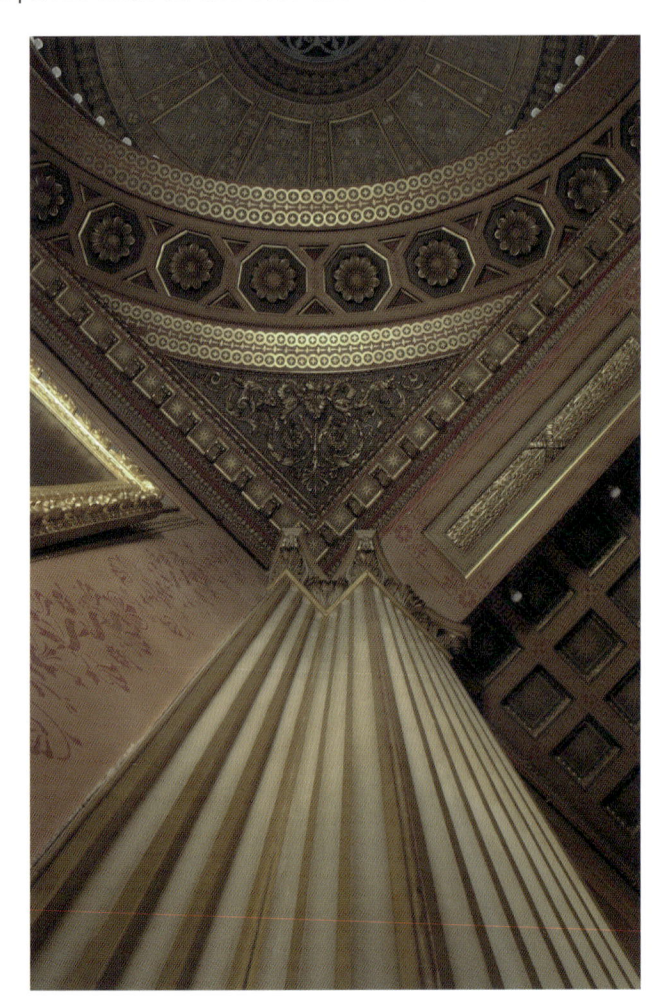

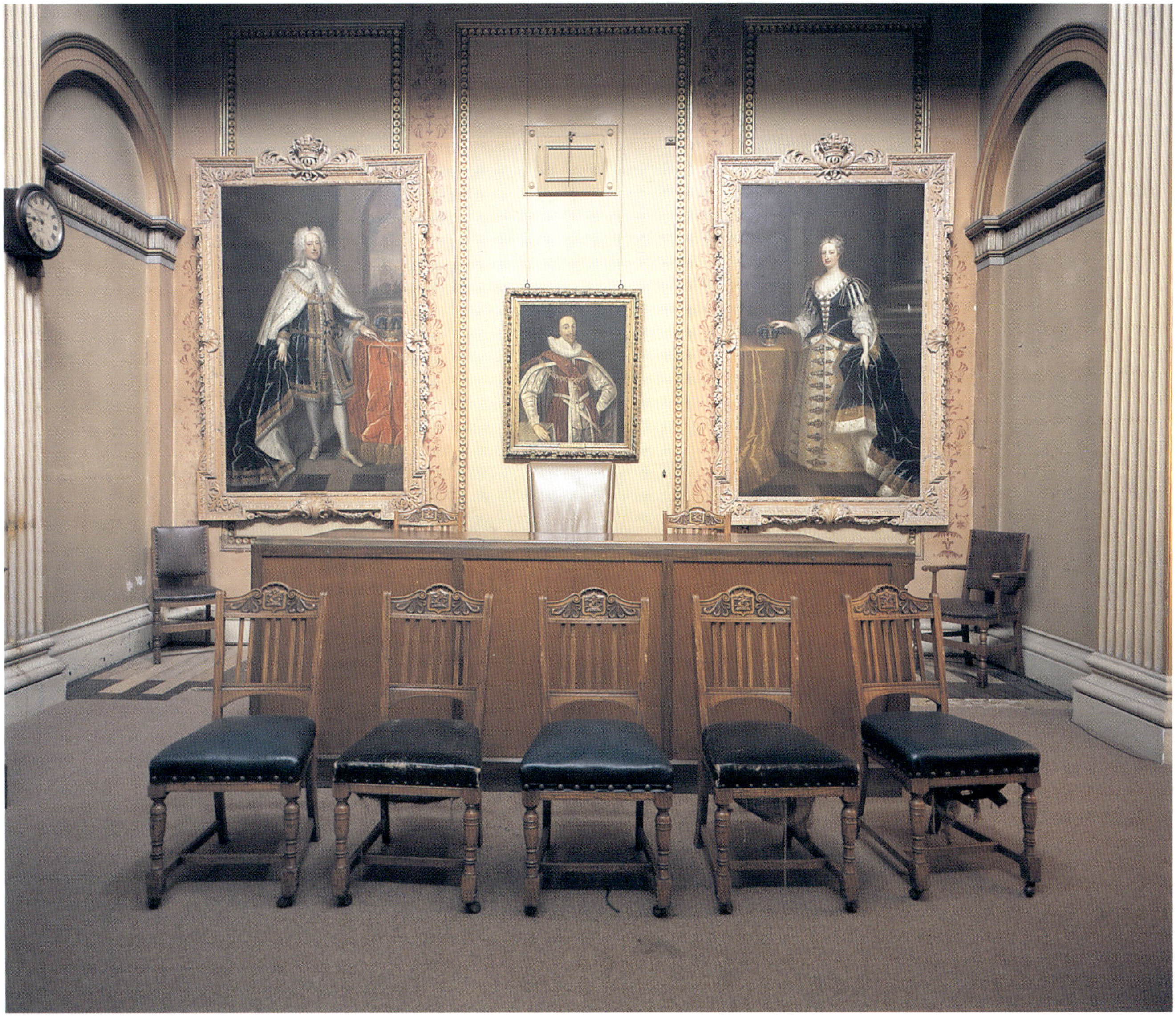

An Invisible Roof open to the Elements

St Nicholas Market

While it is very satisfying to see John Wood's splendid Corinthian cloister at the Exchange fully engaged with St Nicholas Market and part of the city's commercial life, that dim, flat roof which the twentieth century clamped down on it is an aesthetic disaster. Wood meant it to be an open-air market and with our climate that was over-optimistic, but the Victorians dealt with the problem far more imaginatively than we have done. In 1872 they brought in Edward Middleton Barry to add a second storey, a nineteenth-century heaven of caryatid angels and round arches supporting a high, glass and iron roof, airy and elegant. Barry's roof was replaced in 1949, but the ranks of caryatids are still there, exposed now to the elements and earnestly supporting nothing. The only way to see them is to ask permission and go up through the council offices.

An Essay in Communication Skills

Everard Building, Broad Street

Broad Street must be one of the most architecturally indigestible streets in Europe. From that absurdly picturesque church, St John's, set over the last surviving city gate at the bottom end of the street, to Sir Robert Smirke's heavy neo-Greek Council House at the top on the corner with Corn Street, it has something for everyone. But Edward Everard's Printing Works openly disassociates itself in form, colour, even street line, from everything around it. Everard, whose name sprawls in gloriously sinuous graphics over the entrance, was one of those rare businessmen who had not only read William Morris' *News From Nowhere*, but earnestly believed that bright colours and a hit-or-miss medievalism could put the beauty back into the industrial scene.

In 1900, with Henry Williams as his architect and W J Neatby producing the faience decoration, Everard delivered this aesthetic heavyweight onto an already unusually overloaded street. Naturally, Bristol has to be proud of it. There is nothing else quite like it. But why has it no successors? Does it work as a city's street furniture? Can one quite narrow façade get away with four entirely different kinds of arch, all aggressively yawning? Henry Williams seems to have had no natural feeling for the continental Art Nouveau, somewhere a German Romanesque is trying to get loose. But the two women in the tiled portraits are more reminiscent of Dante Gabriel Rossetti's languorous Pre-Raphaelite models or perhaps the *femmes fatales* of the Symbolist artists, while the two faience printers – Morris and Gutenburg, who both designed their own alphabets - are Arts and Crafts in their bold, linear outlines. Was that perhaps the style where Everard and Morris' vision of a clean, kindly new Britain would have been most happily realised?

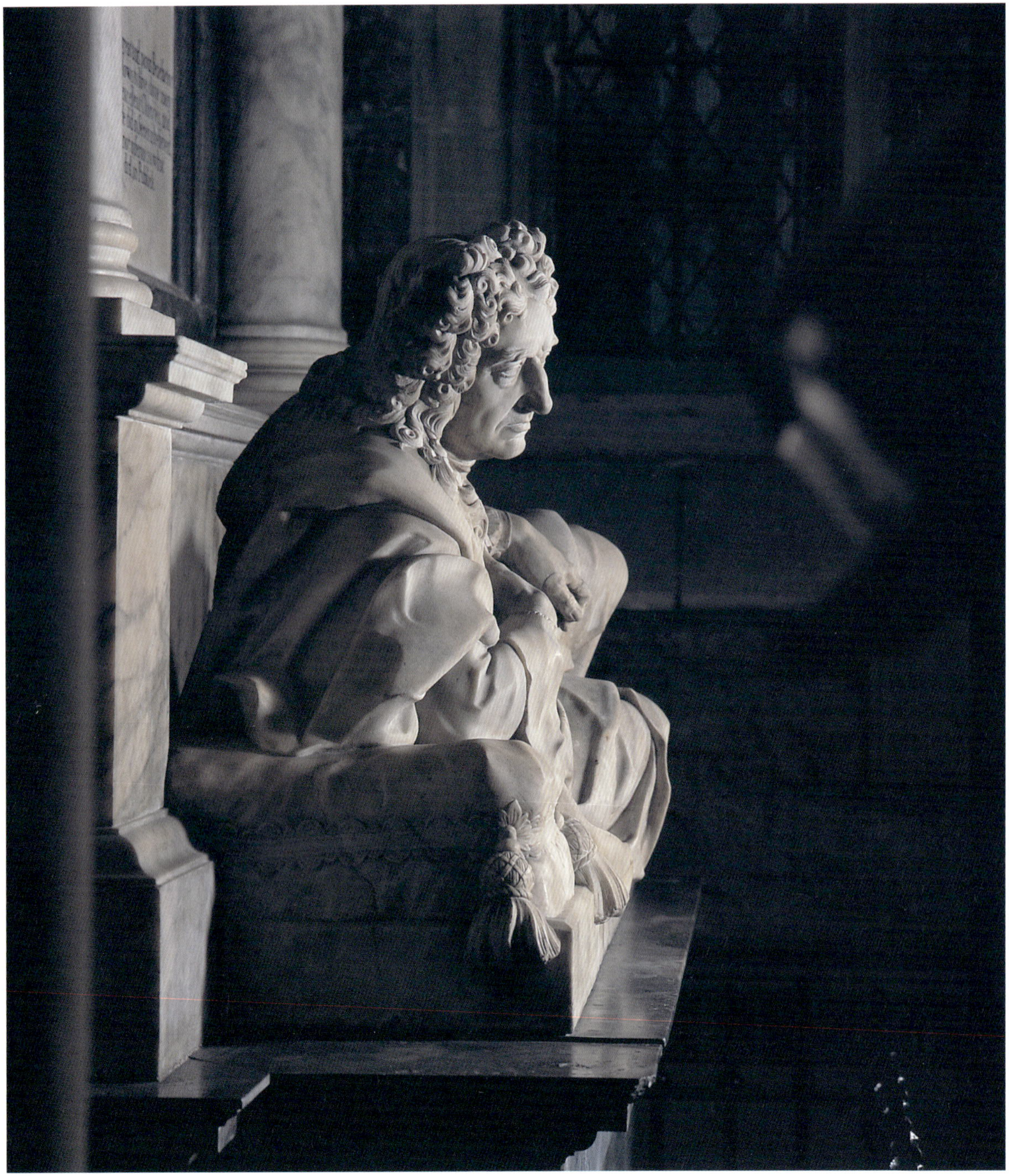

A Politically Incorrect Monument

All Saints, All Saints Lane

With no fewer than eleven Bristol streets and a concert hall named after him, and that attractively irresolute statue of him in the Centre, it could be said that the city has done Edward Colston proud. But then with two schools and an almshouse owing their foundation to him and at least ten churches benefiting from his generosity, he did earn Bristol's gratitude more than most have done. It is only in the last ten years of acute political correctness that Colston's name has become an embarrassment. He did launch the city's eighteenth-century prosperity by breaking London's previous monopoly of the slave trade, leaving it open to the ruthless enterprise of Bristol and Liverpool merchants. So, in an age when someone has to be held responsible for every crime, accident or disaster, the blame for Bristol's most wealthy century has fallen on those frail old shoulders.

The architectural frame for Colston's superb 1729 funeral monument in All Saints was designed by James Gibbs and the recumbent figure was carved by John Michael Rysbrack, though the monument is signed by the local architect and statuary, Michael Sidnell, who probably erected it after it was sent down from London. All Saints is not even a church now, just a consecrated diocesan office, so one of Bristol's greatest art treasures offends no one. Colston reclines grave, dignified and serenely undisturbed by death. If anyone should be confident about his fate in the after-life it is this man; forget the slave trade, remember those schools; what a balancing act for St Peter to weigh up! The marble folds of the monument and the profile of the head are immaculate and sharp. 'Look behind me, count the sermons I have endowed in perpetuity', he seems to be saying, and then comes that splendidly suggestive inscription, leaving the verdict all to us but with no precise evidence: 'This great and pious Benefactor was known to have done many other excellent Charities, and what He did in Secret is believed, to be, not inferior, to what He did in Publick'. Make your judgement on that if you can.

The Tramp as Disciple

St Nicholas, St Nicholas Street

This figure, though almost life-size, occupies a very small corner at the bottom right-hand of the central panel of William Hogarth's giant triptych which he painted for St Mary Redcliffe church in 1756. The left-hand wing of the triptych illustrates the Sealing of the Tomb in the Garden of Gethsemane, the right-hand shows the three Marys at the empty tomb on Easter morning and the huge centrepiece has Christ ascending into the heavens from Bethany with St Peter and the other disciples marvelling at the sight. This photograph, by concentrating on one single figure, proves just why Hogarth never became a great religious artist. He was always drawn to the seedy, ugly side of life, seeing himself as a painter born to mock folly and ridicule vice. Ask Hogarth to paint a crowd of drunken revellers or corrupt politicians and he responds with a telling show of brutish faces, leering mouths and squinting eyes. The trouble was that he could not tear himself away from that line of harsh comic exposure, hence this figure of the kneeling disciple. His bent, pug nose, rough, black beard and eye with far too much white showing, all suggest that Hogarth went looking for a model in some dockside tavern, or picked up a willing tramp. That should not put you off searching out the Hogarth altarpiece. If it is not a great painting it is a very fine one, and its present circumstances give it an added charm of the bizarre. It hangs lowering over a busy office full of desks and filing cabinets in what was, until a few years ago, St Nicholas Church and City Museum by Bristol Bridge. No one knows what to do with it. St Mary Redcliffe don't want to obscure their garish twentieth-century stained glass by re-instating it as an altar-piece; Bristol City Museum and Art Gallery, who are the real owners, have no suitable space, and it costs less to insure it where it hangs now than to roll it up, cart it away and then have to restore the cracks. There is something very Bristolian about all this: a city of supposed art lovers with no interest in the most remarkable work ever painted for them.

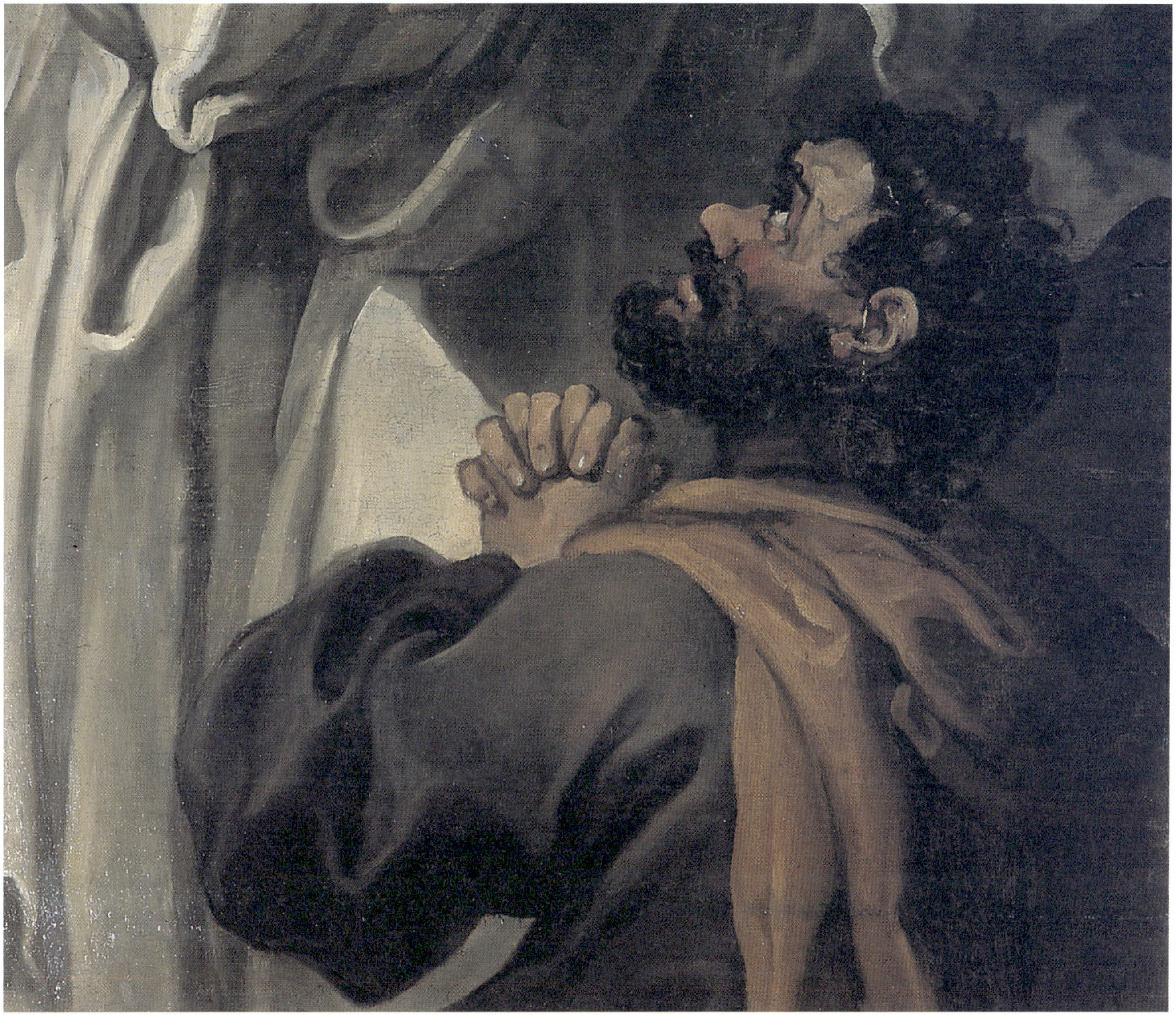

A Bridge Too Far

Rupert Street

This dreadful fragment deserves to be spot-listed and preserved as a monument to pig-headed municipal planning. A slimy stalactite of dripping concrete dangles from the broken ledge where a long bridge was intended to vault across Lewin's Mead to the plaza on which St Bartholomew now rides his bronze horse. Safe from the traffic hurtling without speed limits below them, the citizens of a Sixties' version of Fritz Lang's *Metropolis* were meant to tread these bridges in the sky inhaling the exhaust fumes and praising the inspired bureaucracy which had elevated them. It was initially the local architects rather than the planners who thought up this ridiculous scheme. In 1959 the Bristol Architects' Forum published *A Plan for Bristol* which advocated the segregation of pedestrians from vehicles, relegating the walkers to unlandscaped concrete galleries flanked by slabs of Brutalist building.

The scheme envisaged a twenty-foot high pedestrian deck over the Centre extending from the Colston Hall to College Green, complete with a massive tower block at the head of St Augustine's Reach. This was to create what the report archly called a 'Venetian Piazza'. Fired by this new intellectual thinking on traffic control and pedestrianisation, the council produced in 1966 a City Centre Policy Report which not only proposed more bridges and walkways, but the wholesale demolition of the existing townscape. Fortunately both schemes faltered, literally in mid-air, and if you look carefully around the Centre you will see several of these abandoned bridges ready to plunge pedestrians into the traffic below.

Hotel du Vin Sugar Warehouse

Lewin's Mead

The Alternative Hotel Company, a firm based in Winchester, has done a commendably sensitive restoration of the sugar warehouse in Lewin's Mead after the building had lain empty and nearly derelict for eleven years. It was in 1728 that the first sugar refinery was opened on the site, one aspect of Bristol's infamous three-cornered trade – Africa with brass goods, the West Indies with slaves and then back to Bristol again with the cane.

Boiler room, engine house and an elegant chimney stack have all survived in an interior courtyard that offers a surprisingly intense industrial landscape against the vast, blue-brick terrace that props up the back of Park Row. Everything closed down in 1831 and the premises hung on as a tobacco and bird-seed warehouse. This slick, transparent hood over the entrance sensibly makes no attempt to match the neo-Georgian brick façade next door. Contrasts are the real Bristol theme.

Metallic Blossom

No 1 Bridewell, Rupert Street

The weakest link in Bristol's attenuated centre is that gloomy chasm of the imprisoned Frome where Lewin's Mead, Rupert Street and The Haymarket are stacked with graceless blocks that darken an urban canyon unrelieved by shops or pubs. When Alec French & Partners came to design No. 1 Bridewell Street in 1987 they had to respond to an irretrievably ruined site and work to the wrong scale in storeys. Richard Lee, the project architect, fought his way out of a near-impossible situation by wedging in an angular block which he then lightened by a cladding of cream 'rain-screen' panels. Paint, that anathema to trendy Brutalist architects, was used in bright red strips to dramatise the fully glazed, seven-storey atrium. The building is an early example of High-Tech in Bristol with its sophisticated energy management system and flexible interior space.

Such a fresh, clean-lined building set within a morass of Sixties' concrete positively lifts the spirits as you walk past it. The atrium is radiantly open to the street and alive with interior balconies. At night it is flooded with light and casts into sharp relief, like some futuristic conservatory, the metallic blossom of a writhing computer tree. Here the architect and his developer have succeeded admirably in making an office building visually accessible to the passer-by. It is a great leap forward in cityscape from those faceless blocks whose towering walls of concrete and mirror-glass windows repel rather than invite. Nothing has since been built in Bristol to touch it for sheer architectural class and neighbourliness.

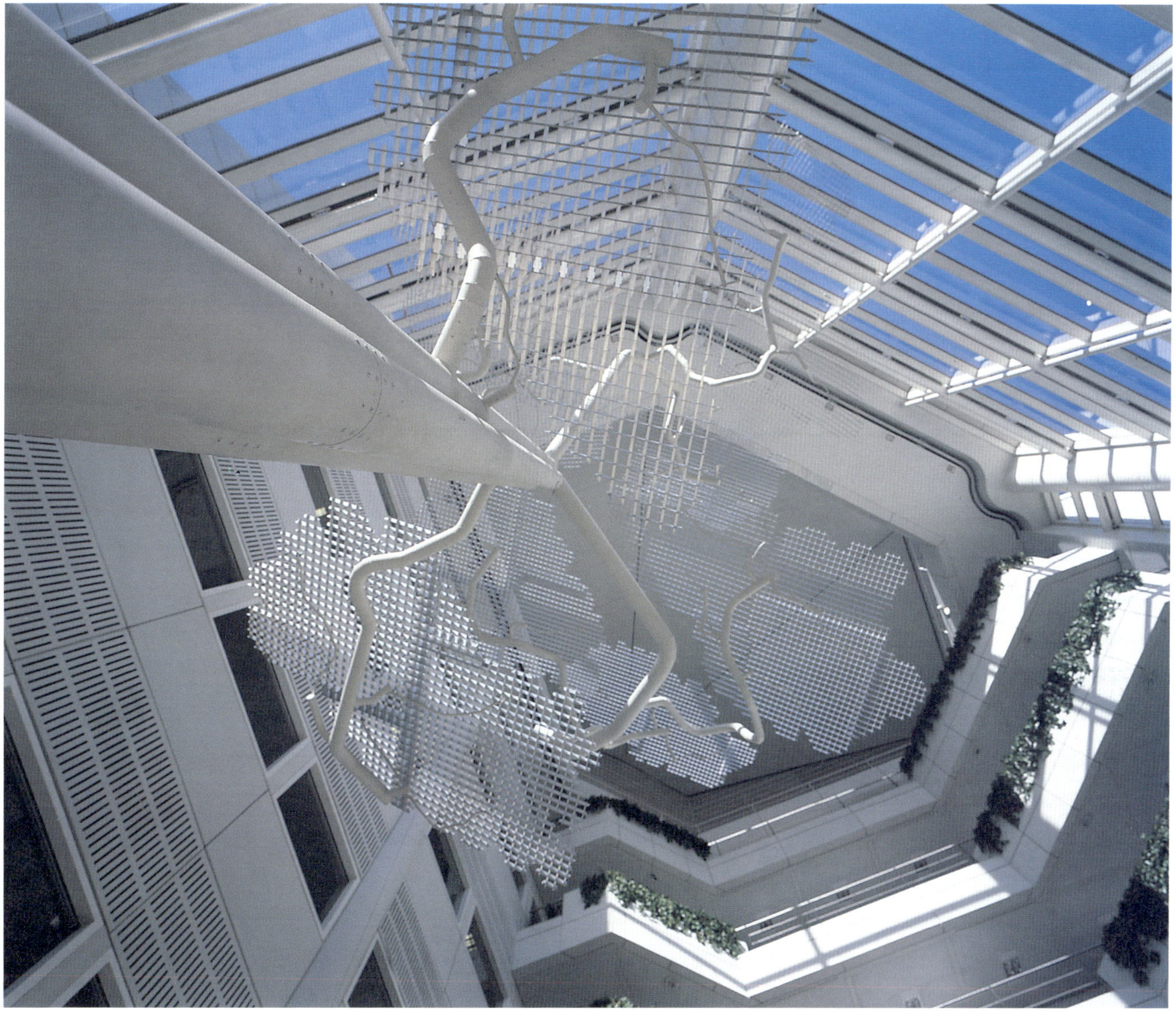

Queen Elizabeth Danced Here

The Red Lodge, Park Row

Bristol does not boast enough. Robbed by the Reformation of the rites of the Catholic Church and the panoply of high altars, the interior decorators of Elizabethan England turned chimneypieces into secular domestic altars, making them the focus of principal rooms. The Red Lodge on Park Row has the finest in England, its only rival a vulgarly over-wrought specimen at Burton Constable in Yorkshire. Sir John Young was determined to host Queen Elizabeth when she visited Bristol in 1574. So, some years earlier, he built his Great House on the site of the present Colston Hall, then as a crowning touch, he went on to raise twin garden lodges on the healthy, breezy slope of Kingsdown: places for private entertainment. Red Lodge is the survivor of that pair and the Great Oak Room with its ribbed plaster ceiling, panelling and towering alabaster and limestone chimneypiece has a fair claim to be the most sumptuous Elizabethan interior left to us.

Nonconformist De-Decorating

Wesley's New Room, The Horsefair

Time ticks solemnly away on the gallery of Wesley's New Room. Whoever designed this lovely, chaotic space (and it was probably the builder, George Tully) had to cope with a constricted site, a limited budget and the need to provide the minister's living quarters as well as the chapel itself. He succeeded brilliantly, imposing a semblance of classical order on the cramped seating arrangements by the six sturdy Tuscan columns that functionally hold it all together. Light has, of necessity, to come from high up as in this side window, but an octagonal lantern manages to flood the place, which could so easily have been gloomy and dark, with a pure Protestant light. John Wesley and George Whitefield bought the site in 1739 and the New Room was completed in 1748. Tully, being a Quaker and a carpenter, might have seemed the natural builder, as opposed to architect, for them to turn to once the Church establishment had barred them from preaching.

One Benefit of Smoking

The Wills Building, Park Row

Sir George Oatley had a vision of Bristol University set high up on its hill above the city and ringed with a crown of twelve great towers, like Camelot revived. Only two of his towers were achieved – the Wills Memorial tower and the Physics Building – but this view of the Wills tower taken from an unusual angle shows how Oatley's immensely solid yet scholarly Gothic was meant to work, rising above tier after tier of apparently medieval buildings. With a confidence in the continued relevance of Gothic to a modern city which is both admirable and also very provincial, Oatley designed his tower as late as 1914 and it was built after the war between 1919 and 1925, a period when the rest of the country was looking to the Art-Deco style and the skyline of New York for inspiration. Not to go inside the great entrance hall that fills the tower's lower stage is to miss one of Bristol's most amazing spaces: seventy-two feet high with fifty-foot windows, like a section of King's College Chapel, Cambridge torn away and used as the entrance to King Arthur's Castle.

Decadent Electroliers

Bristol Museum and Art Gallery, Queen's Road

Bristol City Museum and Art Gallery is not an intensely loveable building. The Museum's own handout describes itself as being 'in a timeless municipal classical style'. Perhaps it is better to have a bad architectural profile than no profile at all. But hanging above the rich, characterless Sicilian white, Cippolino green and Pavanazzo black marbles of Sir Frank Wills' heavy entrance hall, the Art Nouveau, which was the true vernacular style of 1899-1904 when it was all going up, has infiltrated in the shape of sinuous copper electroliers. Originally there were eight of them; now there are four and even these have lost their third tier, which is a pity. But with their broad heart-leaf shapes they still lend a touch of style that can stand up to the battered old aeroplane hanging alongside them.

The Wreck of an Architectural Leviathan

Pro-Cathedral, Park Place

The Roman Catholic diocese of Clifton's first design for a cathedral was a supremely impractical classical scheme of 1834 by the Bath architect, Henry Edmund Goodridge. Not only was it almost entirely without windows, but its giant Corinthian columns soon proved too heavy for the brittle limestone on which its foundations were laid. Its chief promoter went bankrupt and the columns stopped abruptly short of the capitals which never materialised. When Bishop Ullathorne was appointed to the diocese in 1843 he asked Charles Hansom, inventor of the hansom cab, to make something of Goodridge's half-built walls and columns.

Hansom threw a low roof over the structure and supported it internally with wooden piers and braces, a cheap, light and ingenious solution with more reference to Victorian engineering than to Christian precedent. Hansom then returned in 1876 to add a wilfully inappropriate narthex in a North Italian Romanesque style of which John Ruskin would have approved. His lovingly detailed narthex was meant to have included a tall campanile but, as usual, the money ran out and the bell tower was never even started. But the colonettes and the carvings of apostles, lions, lambs and ritual beasts were full of vitality and the whole composition looked well from Queen's Road. When the Catholics moved out to the new cathedral on Pembroke Road in the 1970s the old building languished, was used occasionally as a set for TV productions, but is now being converted into student accommodation. Until the students arrive to take up residence Bristol still has its unique Lombardic Romanesque car-park.

Animal Iconography for Philosophers

Brown's, Park Row

The snarling lion and goat's head rising out of acanthus leaves on the capitals which support the lower cornice of Brown's Restaurant are a reminder of the richness originally intended by the architects, Archibald Ponton and John Foster, for the Museum and Library of the Philosophical Institution when it was begun in 1867. The younger Foster's name is always attached to the design, but its uncompromising Venetian Gothic arches, needle-sharp and defiantly un-English, prove that it was Ponton, a committed follower of John Ruskin, who was the presiding partner when the building was projected. Anyone who doubts this should study Ponton's Avon Insurance Building in Broad Street and his masterpiece, The Granary on Welsh Back. It is, nevertheless, a water-colour signed by John Foster which records the subtle play of Ruskinian colour and carving which should have completed the Museum.

The building has lost the soaring spires of the shrines that once lightened its angled corners, and its niches never received the saints' statues that would have enriched them. The upper cornice was not given the leaf carvings and animal heads which survive on the lower, and west-country weather has decayed the original Gothic parapet, as it has dimmed the colour contrasts of the masonry. The only way to experience the façades that Ponton intended for Bristol is to travel to Padua and enjoy the Loggia Amulea in the Prato della Valle of that city, for that was his inspiration.

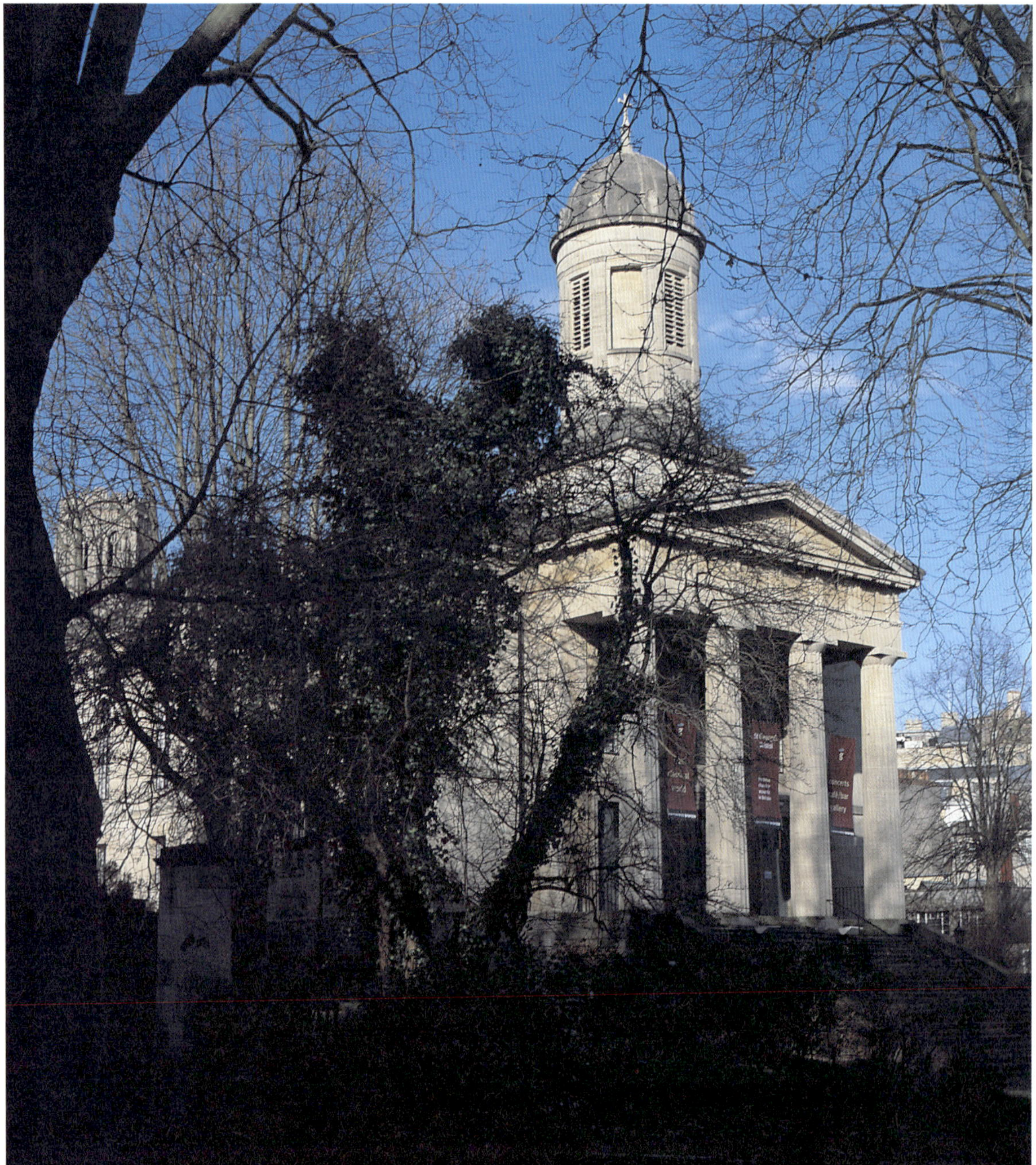

A Grecian Backside on Brandon Hill

St George's, Great George Street

St George's, Brandon Hill seems always to have been something of an embarrassment to the Church of England. Commissioners' churches, of which St George's is one, were supposed to be built to provide worship for the new industrial suburbs where the workers were falling into the grip of Methodism. Brandon Hill could never be described as an industrial suburb, but the middle-class residents of its new Georgian terraces found their small parish church of St Augustine the Less on College Green beneath their dignity, so somehow the Parliamentary Commissioners' money got subverted to the building of St George's.

Robert Smirke, architect of the British Museum, was responsible for the church, which was built in 1821 as a chapel of St Augustine's. For his Bristol church he used exactly the same design as that for St James's, Hackney, only there the church is standing on level ground and not looking as if it were trying to pull back from sliding downhill, as St George's does when viewed from Great George Street. That tremendous Doric portico, severely and accurately Greek without bases to its columns, is an empty gesture leading nowhere at the east end of the church. The real entrance to the west, on Charlotte Street, is a more subdued affair.

Smirke's interior was extremely plain and Protestant, little more than a preaching box to seat, with the galleries, a congregation of 2,000. Yet soon after it became a proper parish church in its own right in 1832 the congregation turned High Church and wanted an interior with a mysterious sanctuary for their ritualistic celebrations. In 1870 George Edmund Street was brought in to make St George's more Anglo-Catholic and he did his best with marble screens, steps and ambos. But slowly the congregation, which never really hit that 2,000 mark, dwindled away and now the building, which is claimed to have the most perfect chamber acoustic in England, has been secularised and is a select concert hall.

Bible Studies for Baptists

Old Baptist College, Woodland Road
That very Edwardian version of an Elizabethan manor house that sits on the corner of Woodland Road and University Walk has become recently the home of the University's Departments of History of Art and Archaeology. Nonconformity is in retreat across Britain and the Baptist Church no longer required a building of that size and discreet dignity to house and train its young ministers, but that is what it was designed for; and today its interiors retain a wholesome air of Arts and Crafts clean living with the grain of its solid oak woodwork in sparing partnership with creamwashed walls. Sir George Oatley evolved the design for the Baptist College over a period of years between 1900 and 1913, its 'Old Basing' red bricks in deliberate contrast to the stone towers he was erecting all round it at the same time. Economy enforced modifications and the College got off to a faltering start. It was completed in 1916 during the First World War, but was not functioning until 1919. It was in the 1920s that colour invaded its austere corridors in the form of the Tyndale Window, twelve dramatic sets of intensely burning glass best described as Arts and Crafts Expressionism.

William Tyndale was not by any stretch of ecclesiastical history a Baptist; born about 1494 he was strangled and burnt at the stake in Belgium in 1536. But as the first and most memorably poetic translator of the Bible that eventually emerged as our King James or Authorised Version in 1611 he was a key figure in the Protestant Reformation. Mrs Robinson, a daughter of the Revd. Frederick Gotch, Principal of the College when it was in Stokes Croft from 1868 to 1883, fixed on Tyndale's life as the theme for a window to the memory of her father and mother. It was designed by her nephew Arnold Robinson and so very much a family affair. In the eleventh and twelfth windows Tyndale is shown in prison at Vilorde near Antwerp still working on his translation with a symbolic lantern shining in the darkness of his cell. The last and twelfth window has this violent image of a dark young man raising another kind of light as he sets a brand to faggots which will soon consume Tyndale's dead body.

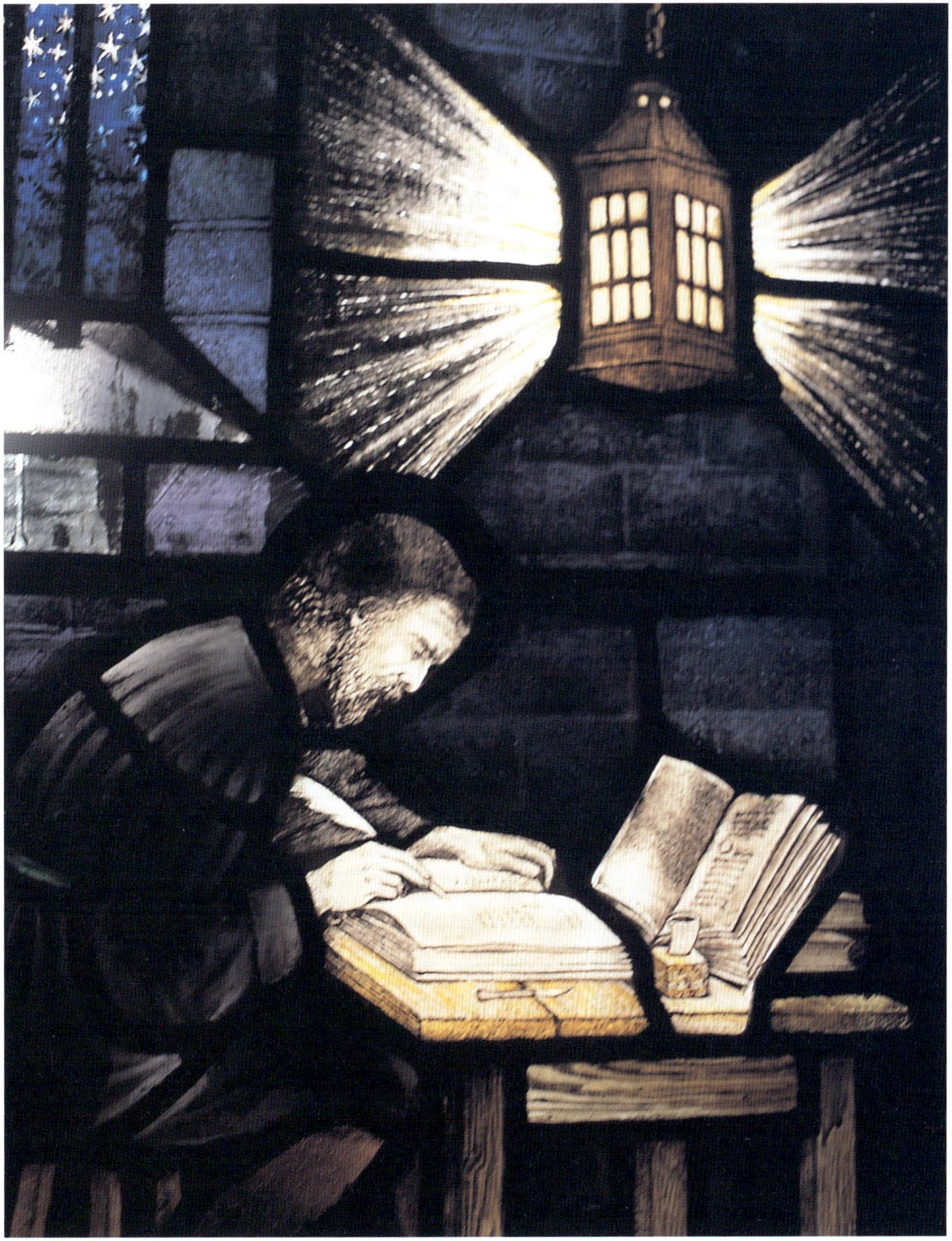

Ill-gotten Rococo

Royal Fort, Tyndall's Avenue

Only those who have actually been into the Royal Fort in Tyndall's Park and seen its stair-hall know what an extraordinary treasure of the European Rococo style Bristol possesses, secretively tucked away behind the Physics tower. A detail like this of one of the great row of nine plasterwork vines which climb its walls is enough to encourage people to take advantage of one of those rare days when the University of Bristol opens the Fort to the public. Like so much of Bristol's best building the Royal Fort was built on second-generation slave-trade money. Thomas Tyndall was of the merchant gentry and he, or his young wife Alicia, had the sense to patronise the Rococo with all its French associations at just that time in the Seven Years War (1756-63) when French fashions were unpopular. Three builder-architects – Thomas Paty, John Wallis and James Bridges – were asked to prepare designs and their three separate elevations were tied together in a model built by Bridges, which is still preserved in the house. Construction began in 1758 under the supervision of Thomas Paty and his team of masons and craftsmen.

The inspiration for the vine trails in the stair-hall must be Chinese wallpaper. Little vignettes of shepherds, floating islands and ruined towers are set at random along the trails, while animals and birds hide among the leaves. Simply to walk up the stairs taking in all the detail is a magical experience of the eighteenth century at its most informal and imaginative. Alicia Tyndall died young in 1764 and there is hardly any decorative detail in the first-floor rooms, so she may well have been the driving force behind the rich, feminine treatment of the ground-floor suite.

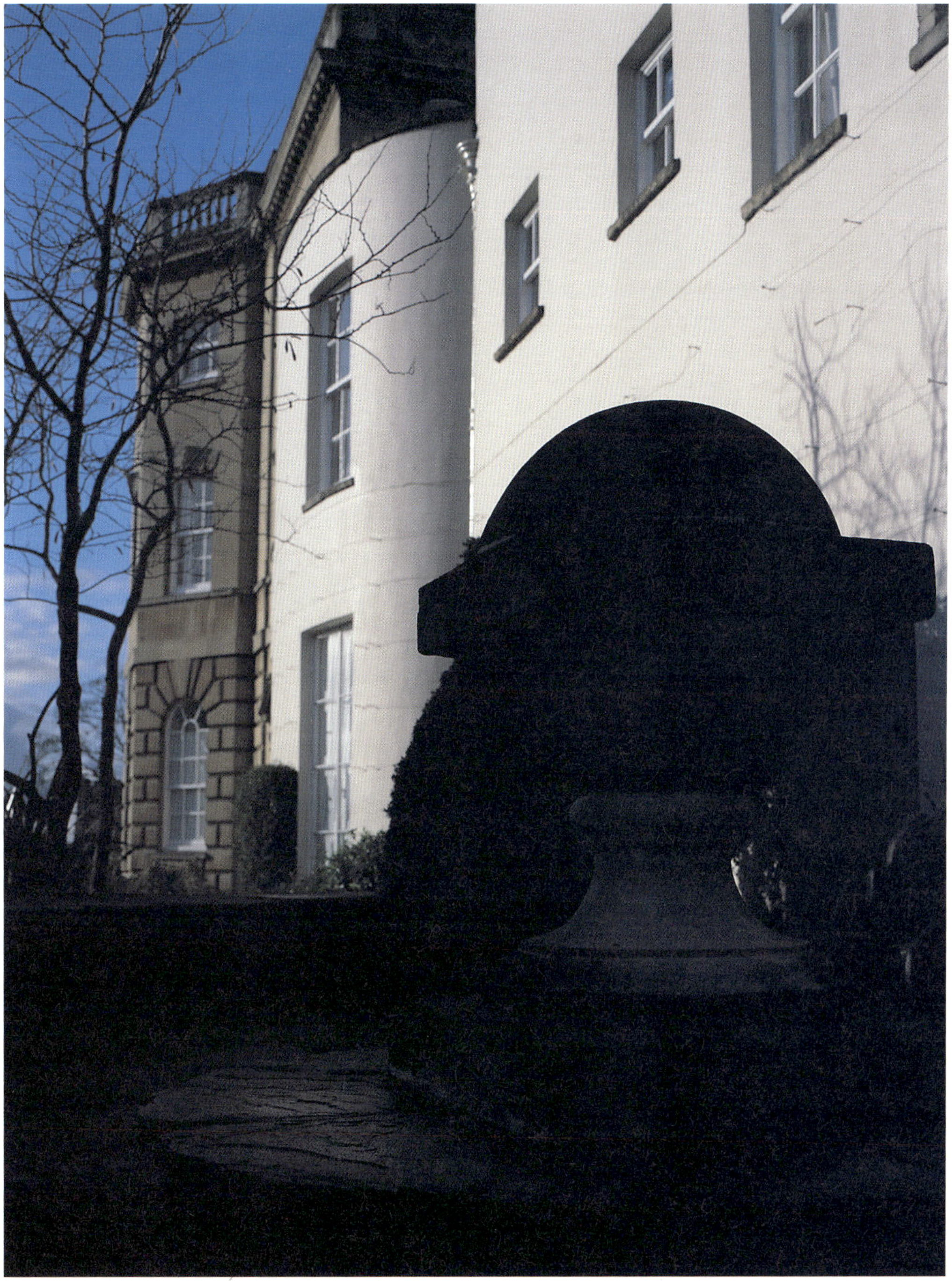

A Twentieth-Century Piazza

Chemistry Building, Cantock's Close

Bristol has any number of eighteenth and nineteenth-century squares, but what only students know is that the city has a mid-twentieth-century square or piazza, high up on the top of Kingsdown, which demonstrates the qualities of modernist architecture in such a ruthless and unflattering way that it should become a standard feature of design pilgrimages. Worried perhaps by the grey and unwelcoming austerity of this new heart to the University, Courtaulds Technical Services turned to the inspiration of abstract art, to Mondrian, to rescue them from a nightmare out of de Chirico. Here is the result: concrete blocks attached to the walls of the Chemistry Building (1962-6) in an apparently random jigsaw pattern. Already some of them seem to be falling off rather than weathering. Could this be the University's opportunity to risk a figurative artist working in colour, to admit that architecture and humanity are not working together in positive accord?

A Study in Doorways

Unitarian Meeting House, Surrey Street and Downleaze

The recessed entrance to the Unitarian Meeting House in Surrey Street off Brunswick Square dates from around 1830; the doorway into number 99 Downleaze, Sneyd Park, boldly proclaims its exact date, 1898, in mannered Arts and Crafts calligraphy. In that sixty-eight year gap there had been a revolution in styling every bit as complete as the twentieth-century move from suburban Tudorbethan to the Bauhaus minimalism of urban tower blocks. On Brunswick Square the ideal is a refined and even emaciated classicism, a linear play that requires light and shadow to enliven it.

At Downleaze the architect Henry Dare Bryan was aiming, with rather too much reliance on stony textures, for the 'Sweetness and Light' suburban charm that Richard Norman Shaw achieved after 1875 at Bedford Park in west London. Now all the emphasis is upon textures and colour contrasts, rough and smooth masonry, panelled wood and an indeterminate air of period antiquity neither Gothic nor Renaissance, but simply allusive by its cherub heads and small hovering angel. This entire road is by Dare Bryan, but all its ingenious variants of gables, recessions, tile-hanging and vaguely seventeenth-century detail of fenestration lacks the lightness of occasional timber and plaster.

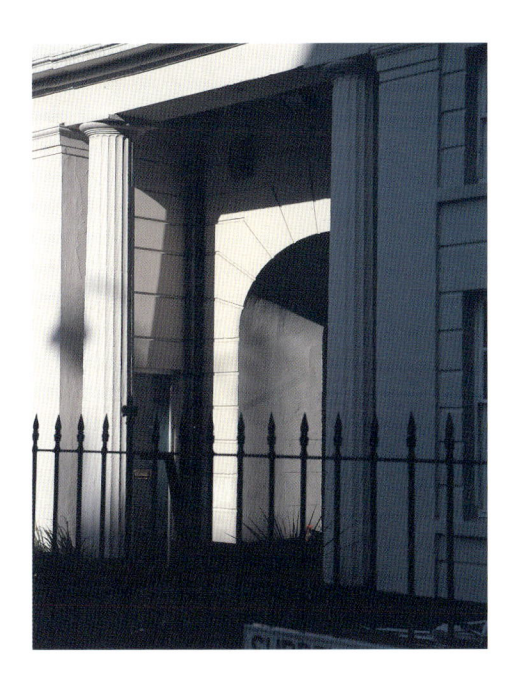

Individuality and Bourgeois Domesticity

Freemantle Square

In the streets and stepped passageways of Kingsdown, Bristol has a polite merchant suburb of multi-coloured stucco and brick with which Bath has absolutely nothing to compare. Up on the 'King's Down' eighteenth and early nineteenth-century classicism went entirely individual. Even here in Freemantle Square, where the houses with their recessed arches on the first floor are conceived as part of a single terrace, a lesene, or dividing pilaster strip, which embodies the assertive apartness of typical Bristol housing, slices down to demarcate one house from another, while pastel colourwash discreetly emphasises the point.

Kingsdown began to boom as a residential area as early as 1742 when John Rocque's map of Bristol showed its roads stepping down from Somerset Street. Development was at its height in the 1770s and 1780s and was always a matter of groups of just three or four houses put up by small firms like the Manleys to make a fast sale, cover costs and then move on to the next enterprise. Freemantle Square was one of the last of these developments, its Regency good manners extending well into Victoria's reign. William Armstrong began it in 1844, perching his square precariously on what had been the earthworks of Prior's Hill Fort, a Royalist Civil War fortification strengthened by Prince Rupert. As a result not one of its sides is at the same level as another, but all share the openness of its central green slope and exemplify now, as when they were first built, that bourgeois ideal of fresh air, privacy and the convenience of breakfasting only ten minutes steep walk from work in the city below.

A New Face in an Old Road

41 Gibson Road

The north side of Kingsdown below St Matthew's church is an intriguing area of Bristol, melancholy with those tall Italianate houses that no Italian would ever recognise as such. It has its star turns. Search out 25 Sydenham Road for its Lombardic Romanesque, or a splendid bay-front half-way down Nugent Hill. Most of the streets have houses only on one side and Gibson Road has houses on neither, just garages and small business premises. That is what makes number 41 so startling – an uncompromising, flush-faced modernist house by Peter Meacock Central Workshop, white, multi-windowed, delicately detailed with a green glass slab for abstract highlighting. There is a construction site two spaces down the road. Gibson Road is becoming upwardly mobile; a sleek new Bristol is on its way, infilling the vacant spaces. Soon we could be quite nostalgic for the old down-at-heel charm.

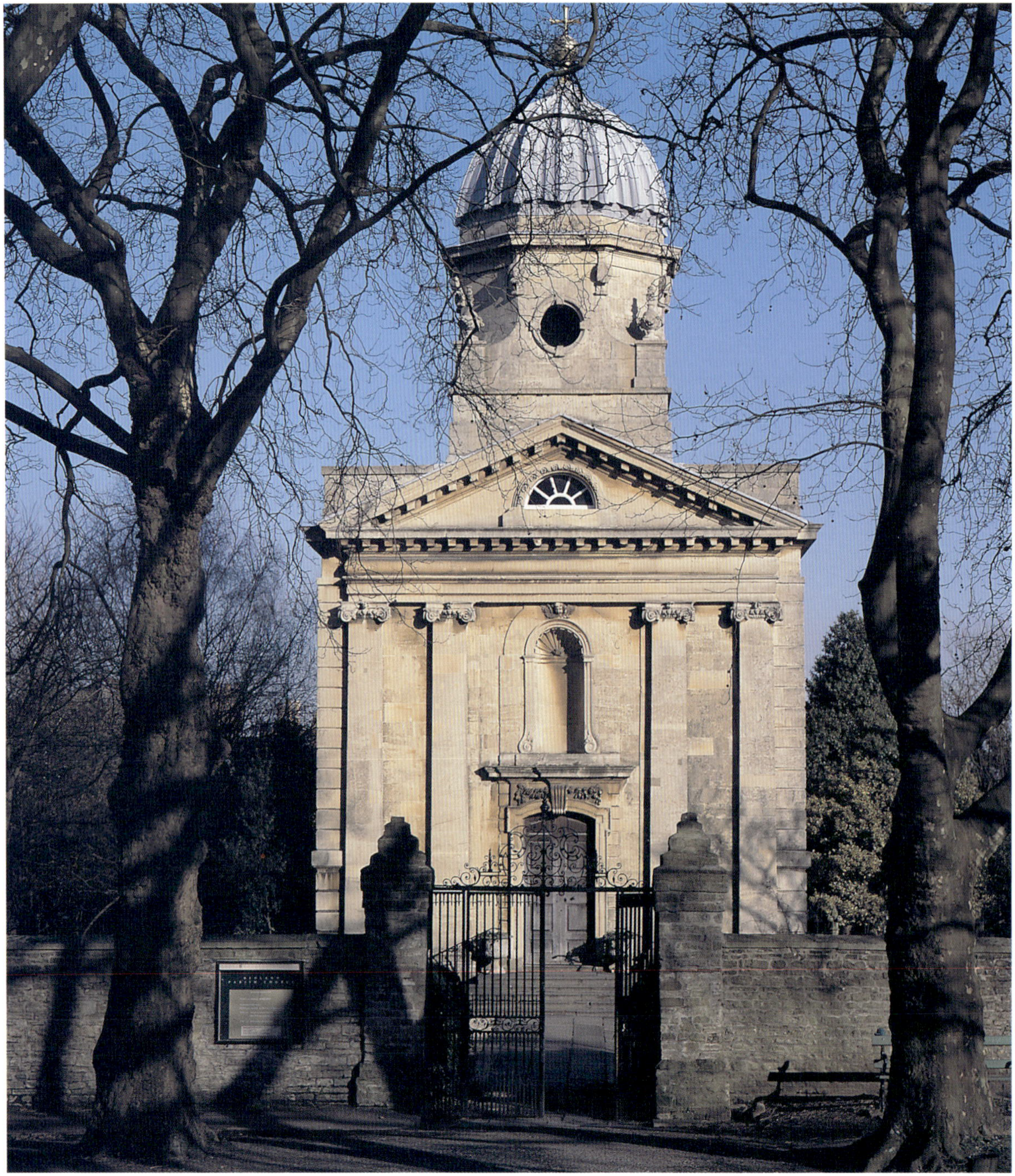

Pattern Book Protestantism

Redland Chapel, Redland Green Road

While there is rich documentation to cover the costing and building of the Redland Chapel by Thomas Paty and his team of craftsmen, there is no certain evidence as to who was its architect. Credit, it seems, must be divided between the Scot, John Strahan, who had designed the neighbouring Redland Court for its owner John Cossins, and William Halfpenny, an irrepressible but unsuccessful Yorkshire designer who had been struggling for work in the Bristol area for several years before he agreed, in May 1742, to supervise Paty's experienced team for the meagre fee of ten guineas. Strahan had died some time before 1742 and the Chapel was not begun until 1741 but, because John Cossins was again the paymaster, Strahan could easily have prepared designs for the building which Halfpenny then had to realise. Looking at the Chapel's handsome entrance front today anyone with a sensitive eye for the distinctive individual signatures of an architect can see that two very different hands have been at work.

The Chapel was completed by 1743, though its elaborate furnishings were being added in 1747 and, while its exterior is the work of Strahan and Halfpenny, its interior is one of several triumphs in the Bristol area of Thomas Paty and his team. The altar is an amazingly exotic composition of harpies and an eagle carrying the gospel, a reminder that, beginning life as a private chapel, it was furnished to a particular private taste. It has never been dedicated in the usual way to a saint and, indeed, was not consecrated at all until 1754. Even now, on Sundays, the Redland Chapel offers the rare experience of a Protestant service conducted in a purpose-built eighteenth-century Protestant preaching space. Finally, for a truly Bristolian touch, see if you can discover at the east end the Chapel's link with the slave trade.

England's First Garden Suburb

Blaise Hamlet, Hallen Road

When John Scandrett Harford of Blaise Castle House commissioned the architect, John Nash, to design nine estate cottages as retirement homes for faithful servants, he could not have dreamed for a moment what a stylistic and social impact his charitable gesture was going to have on England. Even now, almost 200 years after Blaise went up in 1811, it is impossible to write about Nash's exploration of spatial form in housing without first making excuses for being charmed by the deliciously bogus picturesque qualities of the buildings. For English cottages to invite this kind of outdoor living, with a seat designed on a curve to encourage neighbourly gossip and to direct the eye in more than one picturesque direction, was unprecedented; and the thatched roof which projects so cosily to soften the rubble walls is entirely functional as a shelter from the rain.

This photograph neatly conveys why the English had shrunk for so long from any such al fresco living, by catching the Hamlet under a rare Bristol snowfall. Nash's cleverest trick was to overload each cottage with a giant range of Elizabethan-style chimneystacks which would not have looked out of place on houses ten times larger. These raise the profile of the little estate from the merely charming to the architectonic, countering the creeper-clad gables and the coy pigeon roosts. It is the chimneys which have encouraged similar cottages to be raised to house or villa size and repeated in garden suburbs at the fringes of towns and cities up and down the country. Even their arrangement around a leafy green, here artfully contoured with slopes and gentle risings, with a winding perimeter path and village pump as a consciously off-centre focus, has been copied in countless cul-de-sacs of suburbia designed to prevent through traffic and create child-friendly areas.

Prefabs for England's Heroes

Merlin Close

This is England's true version of the Bauhaus spirit revealing itself roughly twenty-five years after the German phenomena, but in very similar circumstances. After the First World War, Germany was economically hard-pressed but urgently in need of new working-class housing. Walter Gropius came up with an austerity building spree of decent, inexpensive flats of a stripped-down functional distinction. With a Labour government in power after the Second World War, England was in exactly the same condition. Returning servicemen were demanding family homes at low rentals in huge numbers and with a minimum of delay. Lord Portal, the Works Minister, was put in charge and he sent off the architect, Alfred Charles Bossom, to America to study the prefabricated houses being erected there.

Prefabs, made in factory units and brought on lorries for quick assembly, usually, as here in Merlin Close, Westbury-on-Trym, in quite small clusters, proved instantly and enduringly popular. Laid down, each in its individual garden plot, with no thin party walls to let the next-door neighbour's wireless set and family quarrels intrude on privacy, they were considered far superior to the pre-war brick, semi-detached council houses. The first 'Portal' houses had a living room, bathroom, kitchen, bedroom and hall, this last consciously designed large enough to store the pram, and there was a separate shed for bikes. To look at they were unimpressive, even mildly ugly; but at the same time they were unpretentious and possessed an endearing functional simplicity. They gave the young families who moved into them the luxury of isolation. This survivor at Westbury (others are being demolished and replaced by modern gabled-roofed versions as I write in March 2001) illustrates how easily the low lines and uncluttered surfaces of a carefully restored prefab takes in the homely clutter of a greenhouse and a family's casual garden impedimenta, a white, wholesome frame to the brighter colours of ordinary living.

A Gentle Gesture Hollywood-wards

Painswick, Old Sneed Park

Whenever a bright green roof of thick Spanish tiles shows up in Bristol's outer suburbs we are in the land of Osbert Lancaster's snidely perceptive cartoons for the pre-war *Daily Express*. With its strangely Cotswolds village name, Painswick in Old Sneed Park is as far as a discreet provincial city's middle class wanted to go in the direction of 1930's trendy Art Deco. No flat roofs of International Modernism for them, and no terrace for sun-bathing, just a shallow balcony where, with luck, the husband could be persuaded to smoke his pipe, and a general horizontality to the lines, including those of the window glazing. Up in the roof is a room for the maid, or would it have been a rumpus-attic for the children? This is the bright, clean wholesome world over which Mr Baldwin presided as Prime Minister, a world of security and traditional values that most of us have been edging back towards ever since.

I Saw Three Ships Go Sailing By

Towerhirst, Circular Road

The sheer drama of the Avon Gorge has nudged at least three centuries of architects, or perhaps their clients, towards including a viewing tower which will command either the coming and going of ships into the Inner Harbour or their arrival at the more stable moorings of the Hung and the King's Roads nearer to the Bristol Channel. There are viewing towers at Goldney, a rooftop widow's walk on a late-Victorian villa on the other side of the Gorge in suburban Leigh Woods, the famous Cook's Folly tower painted by numerous eighteenth-century artists and Edward Southwell's Penpole Lodge at Kingsweston. This example at Towerhirst, where the Circular Road swings closest to the sheer cliff edge just up from Cook's Folly, is a particularly uninhibited example. Anyone taking the stairs to the tower would have enjoyed the final surprise view of the Gorge after a dark, windowless climb up a narrow stairway. The half-timbering is caught up again in stone, tile and plaster on the main body of the house suggesting that the tower was added by a later, Edwardian owner to what was originally a relatively retiring early-Victorian villa.

The Nautical Equivalent of a Keep Left Sign

Navigation Lantern, Avon Gorge

Would any sizeable ocean-going craft try, in this day and age, to come up the Avon Gorge at night? It seems unlikely; but if they ever did the marker lights are still there to warn them of yet another sharp bend in the channel, and each one has its iron access ladder for inspection visits and for small boys to use for climbing practice. Like the steam crane on the harbour wall they make John Piper's point about the strong visual character of any artefact designed to deal with shipping and the sea.

Too Little and usually Too Late

Cumberland Basin, Cumberland Basin Road

Knocking the navigational records of the Merchant Venturers, those wonderful dinosaurs of the late Middle Ages, perhaps the last truly influential medieval guild, has long been a favourite Bristol sport. But to be fair, with a forty-foot tidal rise and several winding miles of narrow waterway up the Avon Gorge, they had their work cut out to keep an essentially inland city as a working Atlantic port. If they had built the New Cut and the Floating Harbour back in 1750 and kept the digging costs down it could have worked; in 1804 it began life expensive and underscaled. There were three attempts to create locks that would cope with bigger and bigger ships – Jessop's, Brunel's and the 1873 one in use today, but Avonmouth was always the logical solution. John Cabot should have cast anchor in Portishead and refused to sail back an inch further. Nevertheless, tidal mud, dank walls, bollards and iron chains compose well for photographers, so we go on pretending.

A Terrace for Bankrupts

Windsor Terrace
While Prince's Buildings course uneventfully on their hilltop, Windsor Terrace stages a series of architectural blunders up to the very edge of a sheer hundred-foot cliff of raw red rock. Windsor remains, nevertheless, the most visually exciting terrace in Clifton with a drama and a distinctive character that nothing in Bath can equal. Not so long ago it had an engagingly run-down air with broken prams and rusty bangers strewn along its weed-grown promenade. But now the money has moved in with buyers eager to command the sensational down-gorge views from the rear windows. Even so the smart, new paint and the repointing cannot conceal the naivety of its would-be grandiose elevations, or make sense of the second thoughts and gross miscalculations behind its giant Corinthian pilasters.

Some Clifton terraces caught the tide of speculative pre-1792 prosperity; Windsor Terrace manifestly missed it. William Watts had made a fortune as the inventor of the process for producing lead shot from his tower by St Mary Redcliffe, and he invested some of it on this entirely unsuitable reach of rocky hillside. Through 1790 and 1791 his money was spent hewing out the cyclopean foundations clearly visible in this view taken from the opposite side of the Avon. Two houses, numbers 5 and 6 in the centre, went up and then the banks crashed affecting all speculative building in Clifton. With the materials still on site, later hack builders like John Drew then had the difficult precedent of constructing a sumptuous Corinthian palace façade, which they catastrophically failed to follow. Only in those centre houses do the capitals connect with the entablature above; the others support nothing, but hang in the façade. And see how the rustication sinks down from Bath stone to crude render as Drew and his builders tried to complete the terrace on the cheap.

A Gesture in the Sky

Clifton Suspension Bridge

What is so stimulating about the Clifton Suspension Bridge is that it was, particularly in 1753 when William Vick, a Bristol wine merchant, first projected the idea and left money to be invested for a bridge across the Avon, entirely unnecessary. Such was the thrusting technological spirit of Bristol at the time that a bridge had to be built simply to prove that it could be done; and in 1753 it couldn't. We beat our breasts today about the failure of Sir Norman Foster's 'Wobbly Bridge' across the Thames to Tate Modern and declare how much better Victorian engineers were than modern ones, but Isambard Kingdom Brunel's exhilarating swoop of metal spanning the Gorge at Clifton took seventy-eight years to think about and then thirty-three years to construct. Work began on the foundations in 1831, but it was not until December 1864 that the bridge was finally completed as a memorial to Brunel who had died of overwork five years before. All that merely to serve a superior middle-class suburb on the Leigh Woods side which only grew up because the bridge was there to make it possible. Walk under it on the towpath to get this view and hope no-one throws a cherry pip over the rail when you are vulnerable.

A Terrace with its own Wood

Prince of Wales Crescent

Despite the fact that almost every house and terrace in Clifton is classical in its styling, it contrives to be in total the Romantic suburb daringly realised: a sophisticated urban experience carried out on the brink of a wilderness. Nowhere can this exhilarating contrast be more completely appreciated than here, where an elegant terrace of semi-detached pairs, linked by what were originally single-storey extensions to the pair next door, is poised on the verge of a headlong woodland of sycamore, rocks, ivy and ferns. Bath was rebuilt under the John Woods, father and son, to impose order on a broad river valley. Clifton was called into being to enjoy the savage prospect of one of England's rare river gorges of near-continental grandeur. Writers of the Picturesque like William Gilpin had made wild nature fashionable with their travel books, and the first surge of terraced developments in Clifton resulted in a Tibetan lamasery of houses facing the warm south and commanding dramatic vistas from their steep, sloping sites.

The Prince of Wales Crescent (now Prince's Buildings), probably designed by Thomas Paty's son William, went up as a speculation by Samuel Powell, and its first houses were being sublet in 1787, three years before Powell unwisely became Proprietor of the Hotwells Spa. He paid the Merchant Venturers £900 a year for the privilege of running the lukewarm, saline pool at the foot of the wooded near-precipice that the Crescent crowns. Yet even in his best year he made only £917 profit on a venture which Bristolians deserted as soon as he charged them 26 shillings a month for entry to the waters. War broke out with France in 1793 and the resultant slump in the building trade ruined many venture capitalists. It was Powell's two already tenanted terraces, this one on top of the Gorge and St Vincent's Parade two hundred feet down below it, that saved him from bankruptcy. Facing south over its private wood and the tidal Avon, the Crescent's balconies have proliferated to indulge owners who wished not to tame Nature but to enjoy it. These were the Bristolians who would value the intellectual soirées of Great George Street where Robert Southey, Samuel Coleridge and William Wordsworth were exploring the possibilities of a new Romantic poetry.

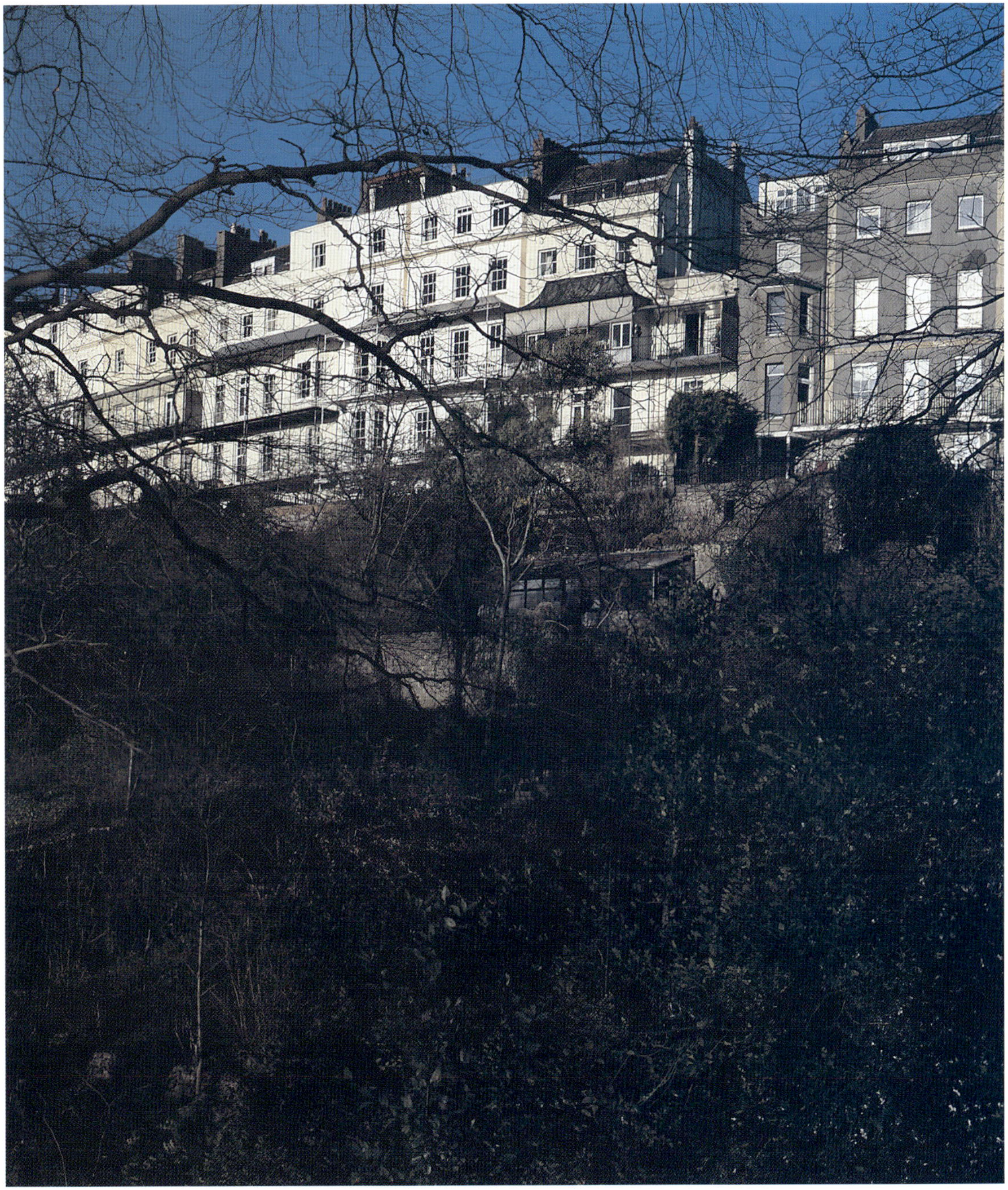

St Tropez-on-Avon

Freeland Place
Bristol is only twelve miles down-river from Bath, but in their approach to classical terracing the distinction between the two cities is that of 'north' from 'south', with Bristol emphatically the warm, southern neighbour. In Bath the terraced houses of the lower-middle classes are as austere and stony as those of their upper-class models. Freeland Place, which linked Clifton with the Hotwells spa, is, in complete contrast, a chant of cheerful individual distinction. Each house is separated from the one next door by a lesene strip and, because they are plastered – far cheaper than an ashlar finish such as the two John Woods imposed upon Bath – they can shine out in a feast of almost Mediterranean colour, rivalling the blue sky behind them. The only mark of designed unity in this terrace of the early 1820s is the quadrant curve by which their cornices and parapets slide rather than step downhill.

Domestic Serendipity on the Clifton Heights

Granby Hill
Pitching steeply down to Hope Chapel Hill and Dowry Square, Granby Hill raises an ordinary block of late eighteenth-century houses to the level of fine architecture by the sheer constraints and improvisations forced upon the builders by the site. If the latest additions to Bristol's building stock along the Hotwell Road are anything to go by, our twenty-first-century response to building on an interesting hillside is simply to remove whole sections of the hill.

Gazebos for Students

Goldney Residences, Goldney Avenue

This is an admirable case of Bristol University being taken by a fit of aesthetic responsibility. The grounds of Goldney House are a significant amalgam of trees, greenery, eighteenth-century garden features and very steep hillsides in the middle of the Bristol-Clifton urban complex. The Goldney Grotto, created over many years by the ladies of the Quaker merchant Goldney family from 1737 onwards, is one of the finest surviving examples of its kind in the country, still ablaze with its original crystals and semi-precious stones, so its immediate architectural surroundings had much to live up to. In the 1960s a decision was reluctantly taken to ease the student lodging situation by building residential blocks on the original orchard of this sensitive site and, though they were given an architectural design award, the nine grey-brick structures clustered around a dark courtyard were not seen as adding to the garden pleasures of the city. Time passed and the need for student accommodation which could be used out of term time, for conferences, increased. In 1993 permission for a new Linbury Court was given but, as a planning gain, the old grey blocks were to be refurbished, linked together and reclad in a style which the Goldney gardens deserved.

The Alec French Partnership was awarded the contract and with David Mellor as the project architect a dramatic transformation was effected. There were already two towers in the garden, both of eighteenth-century date. Taking his cue from these gazebos Mellor devised a whole new battery of light-hearted stair turrets of open balconies with impudent caps, vaguely Chinese, as if some oriental gentleman were politely raising his hat to the city. The new sloping court created between these and Linbury Court is open yet neighbourly, producing a safe environment with interior and exterior views. This new complex is modern but related more to its site than to any particular school of modern design, a sensitive response to a difficult and demanding situation. If only all architects would work to the same civilised restraints.

Clifton's Linear Park

St Andrew's Walk

This is the long pergola of pleached lime trees under which the grieving Juliet Stevenson walked in the film *Truly, Madly, Deeply*. Cinema buffs will remember Alan Rickman's playing of an affectionate husband, a cellist, killed in an accident but left as a reluctant ghost haunting his much loved wife in their house in nearby Pembroke Vale. The Lime Walk was laid out in Church Close, an extension to the existing parish graveyard, after a new St Andrew's church, the third church on its site, was built by the elder James Foster after 1819. This new, arrow-straight, paved path protected by wrought-iron Regency railings and lit by graceful overthrows, provided a direct route to Clifton parish church from the houses in nearby Richmond Place. House values of any new development always went up if there was a church close by to offer spiritual refreshment and a round of polite social activities. St Andrew's and its romantic linking pathway would later become the catalyst for the creation of Victoria Square. The church was gutted by German bombs on the night of 24 November 1940, but its tower, which survived the destruction, was needlessly demolished in 1958. Now the walk leads through the delicately decayed graveyard with its yews and towering cedars, past one wonderful Victorian tomb with six mourning angels, through an elegant gateway to a dramatic surprise view out over the Avon valley.

Convex upon Convex upon Concave

The Paragon
John Drew, the builder who perpetrated the enchantingly dreadful wings to Windsor Terrace in Clifton, managed to erect the first ten houses of The Paragon on the mini-precipice above Windsor before he went bankrupt in 1813. Stephen Hunter, who completed the Paragon with these satisfying Greek Revival porches, probably refaced the entire street side of the terrace and devised that wonderful return house at the end, which can only be viewed properly if you are on a hang glider or microlight. There is a theory that the pioneer modernist architect, Berthold Lubetkin, retired to Clifton so that he could enjoy the clever spatial counter-flow of terrace and porches afresh every morning.

Mousehole or Clifton?

113 Princess Victoria Street

This is not, contrary to appearance, a picturesque corner of a Cornish fishing village. It is 113 Princess Victoria Street, the most charmingly down-beat and architecturally various road in Clifton, with not a single grand terrace, just mews premises and artisan infilling behind Royal York Crescent and Caledonia Place. The blue plaque marks the improbable residence here from 1969 to his death in 1990, of the white hope of English International Modernism in the 1930s, Berthold Lubetkin. Russian-born and Paris-trained, Lubetkin made his name with the Penguin Pool at London Zoo followed by two dashingly geometrical blocks of flats – Highpoint I and II – in Highgate (1933-8). If it seems a cop-out for an avant-garde designer to retreat to this modest, late-Regency house, remember that the modernists claimed to be taking off, with white walls and simple fenestration, from where the Regency left off around 1830.

A Gothic Nunnery in Classical Clifton

St Vincent's Priory, Sion Hill

Some architects accumulate whole chapters of praise and analysis for their ingenuity in coping with the problems of a restricted site, but while most writers on Clifton will drop a word of amused condescension for the anonymous designer of St Vincent's Priory, no one sets it in its actual context of the lean, miserably uninspired but entirely typical Clifton houses next door. Compared with these - the safe Clifton average of domestic expression - the Priory is a dazzling innovation of design with so much achieved within such spatial limitations and not a bored, predictable line in one of its four storeys. The possibilities which this house suggests accumulate the longer it is considered. What complexities of invention and individual expression a single street could contain if the English habit of dutiful conformity could be cast aside on every house! This is not an impossible dream. Belgian house owners of the 1890-1910 period would not buy a house if it was a mere echo of its neighbour. A walk around the middle-class suburbs of Brussels will reveal literally 6,000 tall, terraced houses, each one unique in its design: doors, windows, gables and carved details twisting and writhing in Art Nouveau originality.

St Vincent's Priory is a Regency building, but most Regency Gothic design plays on the predictable near-rectangularity of the Perpendicular Gothic period (1350-1550). Whoever conceived the Priory, as a response to the supposed call of a medieval anchorite which now lies in its cellars, had the wit to see that the lean, spare elegance of the Regency house interacted far better with the slender lancet windows and bold figurative carving of Early English Gothic (1180-1280). So perceptive and scholarly was the lost minor genius that he took casts of carved figures from the north porch of St Mary Redcliffe and used them as models for the animated supporters that reach up beneath the bold, projecting bow of the Priory's first-floor drawing room and then again below a reflecting curved cornice at attic level. Unlike the houses next door the Priory never allows the eye to predict a pattern of fenestration: greater supporting lesser. Its windows billow out, swell, recede and soar; the entrance door is mysteriously concealed. Implicit in this house is the great Victorian rejection of classical propriety and the nation's adoption of stylistic ecleticism as the norm.

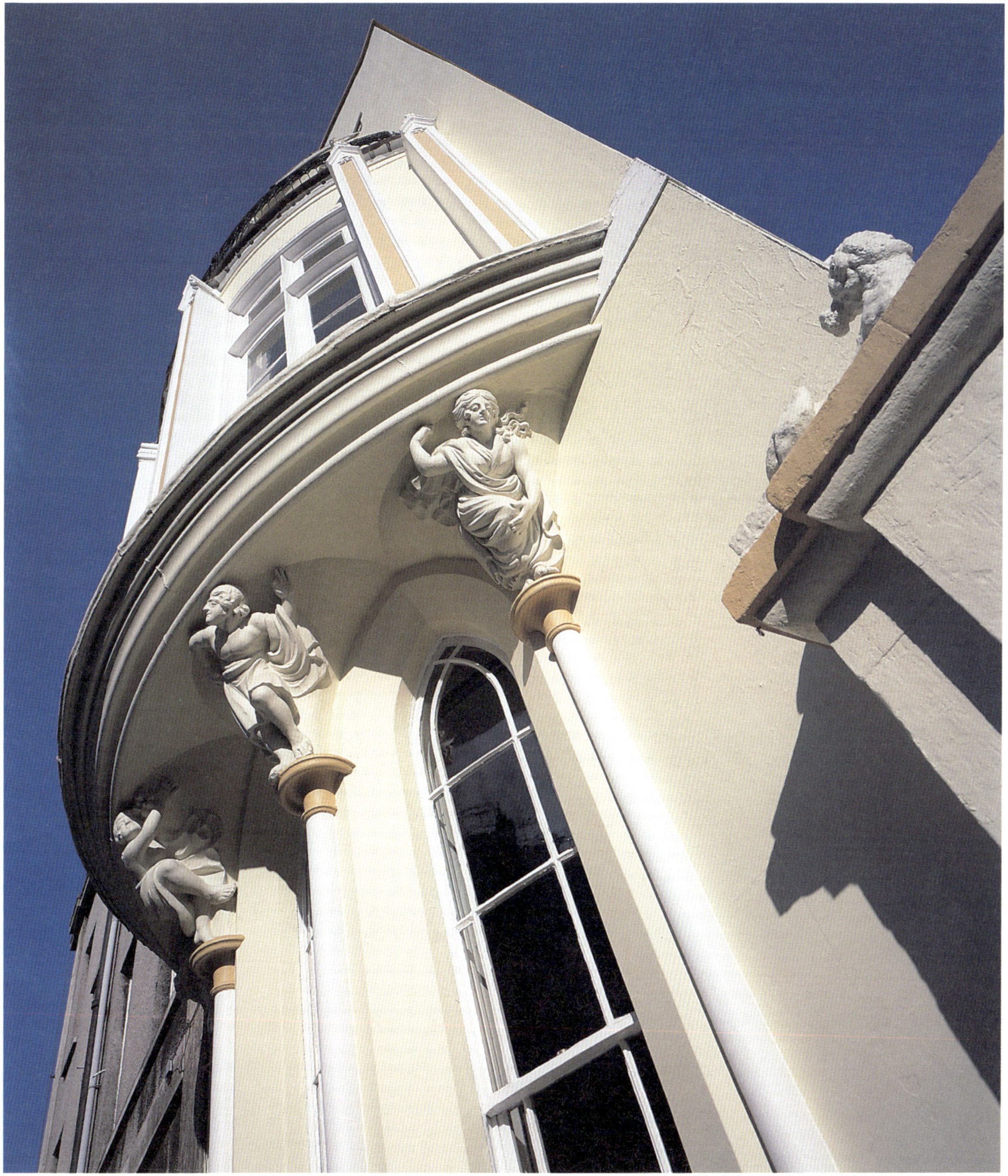

Paris, Clifton

Avon Gorge Hotel, Prince's Lane

No, this is not part of the ruins of Palmyra, nor is it a dilapidated section of a one-time high class Belle Epoque bordello. In 1893 the Merchant Venturers gave permission for the Clifton Rocks Railway to be cut through the cliffs to connect the Hotwells and passengers on the railway from Avonmouth with upper Clifton, provided a hydropathic institute was built at its summit. The conditions were agreed, a pump room was completed in 1894 with a ballroom, whose walls these melancholy caryatids adorned.

The Grand Spa Hotel, now the Avon Gorge Hotel, was ready for business in 1898 and for some thirty years the Rocks Railway flourished. But the hydropathic institute and pump room languished. The water pumped up from the Sion Spring below in the Gorge to the St Vincent's Rocks Hotel on the other side of the street grew cooler and, apparently, less effective. Now these graceful autumnal figures remain to recall a lost time of Edwardian opulence and Bristol's idle rich.

Bays, Bows and Balconies

Sion Hill

Classical order and classical symmetry are all very well, but anyone who takes a critical walk along Bennett and Russell Streets in Bath will find how dull such qualities are when unrelieved by the lively pattern of ironwork and balconies. So many of Bath's buildings were only lodging houses where the proprietors had little inducement to spend on extras. Bristol, in contrast, was a wealthy merchant city where house owners were at least as interested in self-advertising as in classical propriety. While Bristol has nothing quite up to the repetitive grandeur of Bath's Royal Crescent, its classical housing has far more variety and interest than that of the refined sister city. On Sion Hill, with the Gorge and the Suspension Bridge to demand appropriately dramatic viewing platforms for each first-floor drawing room, the bulge of the bow fronts has been picked up and exaggerated to give a most satisfying rhythm of rotundity. The houses date from the 1780s when Clifton was still a village on the edge of a spa – the Hotwells by the river below.

Eighteenth-Century Cinemascope

Camera Obscura, St Vincent's Rocks

This, captured by mirrors upon a broad white concave screen, is the Avon valley viewed in the dark upper room of the camera obscura tower on Clifton Down. Until a fire in 1777 the building was a windmill powering a snuff grinder; but then an entrepreneur saw the potential for offering thrilling, by the quiet standards of the day, visual entertainment for patrons of the popular spa down at the Hotwells. A camera obscura made a perfect focus for an afternoon jaunt and people came flocking to marvel at a moving image with trees blowing in the wind, carriages bowling along roads and lovers romping in the bushes. Long before Fox Talbot invented photography here was the cinema of the day. Even now it has real period charm, particularly if followed up by the Gothic excitement of dark winding steps down beneath it to the Hermit's Cave that looks out over the Gorge.

An Architectural Tiller Girl

Camp House, Clifton Down

This must have been Charles Dyer's next architectural job after he had designed Litfield House, just up the hill, in 1830. His father, George Dyer, was a fashionable Bristol surgeon and his connections would have earned Charles the commission, in 1831, to design Camp House for Charles Pinney, who was mayor of the city in that year of the infamous Bristol Reform Riots. Pinney escaped from the mob at the old Mansion House on Queen Square only by crawling along a gutter and breaking into an attic window of the Custom House next door. He lost most of his linen, glass and china and would have been glad to have Camp House to retreat to in the calm of Clifton. Dyer's design is busy. The double-decker portico lunges forward to the road with un-Grecian enthusiasm, he has deployed his joke balustrades of miniature Doric columns here as at Litfield, and the window architraves contradict each other on every floor. As a final kick in the teeth of expectations, Dyer has set another Doric porch casually at the side where you will find his signature. Fans of this extrovert architect should seek out Oakfield House on Oakfield Road as that was probably Dyer's first experience in a home-grown neo-Classicism.

All My Own Work

Litfield House, Litfield Place

Not many architects are so proud of their buildings that they sign them, but Charles Dyer's carved signature, along with the date 1830, is here on the entablature of the porch to Litfield House, the first of that resonant chain of classical villas that overlook the Downs and the Gorge on Bristol's most exclusive road. You can also find his signature on Savile Place and high up on the pediment of the Victoria Rooms. Whether Dyer should have been quite so self-satisfied is another matter, as Litfield is an instance of a Bristol provincial architect going stylistically over the top in an effort to impress his client, the wealthy Bristol merchant, Henry Bush. The porch of coupled columns illustrated here is severely neo-Classical with a bare two inches of fluting to relieve its dramatic *entasis*, or fattening. But this pure Grecian introductory note is almost overwhelmed on the façade behind it by a display of fruity Roman detail: coupled Corinthian pilasters with oddly compressed capitals, heavy window architraves and inelegant stone balustrades. Inside, the consulting rooms have rich plasterwork ceilings and the waiting room has imposing scagliola Ionic columns. Henry Bush died in 1857 and is buried on the north-west side of St Andrew's Walk in Clifton. Litfield House is now a private medical centre, a fitting use for a building designed by the son of a surgeon.

From Mews House to Bauhaus

Bauhaus, Litfield Road

Tucked away in Litfield Road, a quiet street below Clifton Green, is this admirable house: proof that the spirit of adventurous and eccentric design was not dead in twentieth-century Bristol. Bauhaus, as it has been renamed recently, was built in the mid-1970s as an exploration of pure white geometrical solids, a return to that European Modernism which émigré architects like Serge Chermayeff and Le Corbusier were pioneering in the 1920s and 1930s. Only the new name is inappropriate. Real Bauhaus building was the German equivalent of our council house estates: accommodation for the workers built on the cheap in the early 1920s, but designed with an elegant economical austerity. The Bauhaus School of Design, founded by Walter Gropius, was an art and architectural co-operative, socialist and subliminally egalitarian.

Our Clifton Bauhaus is an aristocrat among suburban villas, manifestly expensive as it is austere and with an air of earthquake-proof solidity. There is a complete lack of motion in its chunky parts that Bauhaus flats could never afford to achieve. After making that minor quibble, the house is intellectually most satisfying and, out of sight there in the mews world of Litfield Road, away from the prevailing classicism of Clifton, it creates its own, sunny Californian ambience. Instead of the all-over imitation concrete finish of whitewashed render which characterised 1930s prototypes, the cubes and rectangles of Bauhaus are dramatised by the clear, dark lines of the jointing to create an architecture of emphatic Cubism, relieved only by the straight lines of the ironwork and an occasional repetitive grid of ventilators. It is rewarding to make a pilgrimage there on a sunny day to enjoy the building's calm, logical planes and then to go down to that mindless jumble of discordant and untalented office blocks which has grown up between Temple Meads station and Temple Way. The contrast between the two sites is a worrying reminder of how low architecture can sink when architects are not directed by patrons of sense and sensibilty but by committees.

Flying Penguins in the Gardens

Zoological Gardens, Clifton Down

The enclosure for seals and penguins at Bristol Zoo is a JM Barrie-wonderland of wrecked ships, rocky outcrops and cascades. It was opened by the conservationist, Dr David Bellamy, and is always crowded with children who scream with delight as the seals dive in and out of the water and the penguins stoically shiver. Underneath the complex is a system of walkways which thread through the waters and give the extraordinarily perverse impression that the penguins are flying in some science fiction sky while actually swimming on the surface.

Ecclesiastical Brutalism

RC Cathedral, Pembroke Road

In 1969 the Roman Catholics finally despaired of making anything satisfyingly diocesan and uplifting out of their pro-cathedral on Park Place. By choosing Sir Percy Thomas & Son as their architects for a trendy modern cathedral - and the 1970s as the decade for their choice - the Catholics got a boldly Brutalist solution to ritual problems. Like its Park Place predecessor it has an undoubted presence and Clifton may have needed a shake-up. Pressed by the Vatican 3 diktat to make a theatre-in-the-round space for the congregation so that everyone could see the high altar, the building is designed in a series of hexagons. This upward interior shot demonstrates that in an era of shuttered concrete and significant abstract shapes even a hexagon cannot be taken for granted. Outside, a chunky concrete typeface had to be devised to convince passers-by that all these angular pylons and semi-flêches really were part of a cathedral and not just functional chimneys servicing a modern factory.

Cinema Paradiso

Whiteladies Picture House (now the ABC Cinema)

The sky rocket tower of the Whiteladies Picture House is a perfect expression of glitzy Hollywood panache on Bristol's answer to California's Sunset Strip. The building, originally projected as an early leisure complex with cinema, dance hall and restaurant all under the same roof, was designed by Henry Latrobe and Thomas Henry Weston in 1920-1. The architects were also responsible for the Cabot Café on College Green, but here they are moving forward stylistically from Art Nouveau towards a fusion of French Beaux Arts classicism and 1920s Art Deco. When the cinema opened in 1921 Betty Balfour was the most successful British screen artist playing roguish Cockney urchins in films like *Mary Find the Gold*, and Sybil Thorndike was just starting out on her Shakespearean film career as Lady Macbeth and Portia. The smash hit of the year was Conan Doyle's *Hound of the Baskervilles* with Eille Norwood as Sherlock Holmes and Hubert Willis as Dr Watson. Even though the ABC is a well patronised local amenity its future as a cinema is under threat at the time of writing (summer 2001). The lavish architectural treatment, particularly around the columned entrance portico and the side wall with its winged wreaths, gives it the air of a minor fantasy palace by Cecil B De Mille and makes it instantly recognisable as a purpose-built cinema. To turn it into a fitness centre would be to deny its important social function and to make a mockery of its distinctive character.

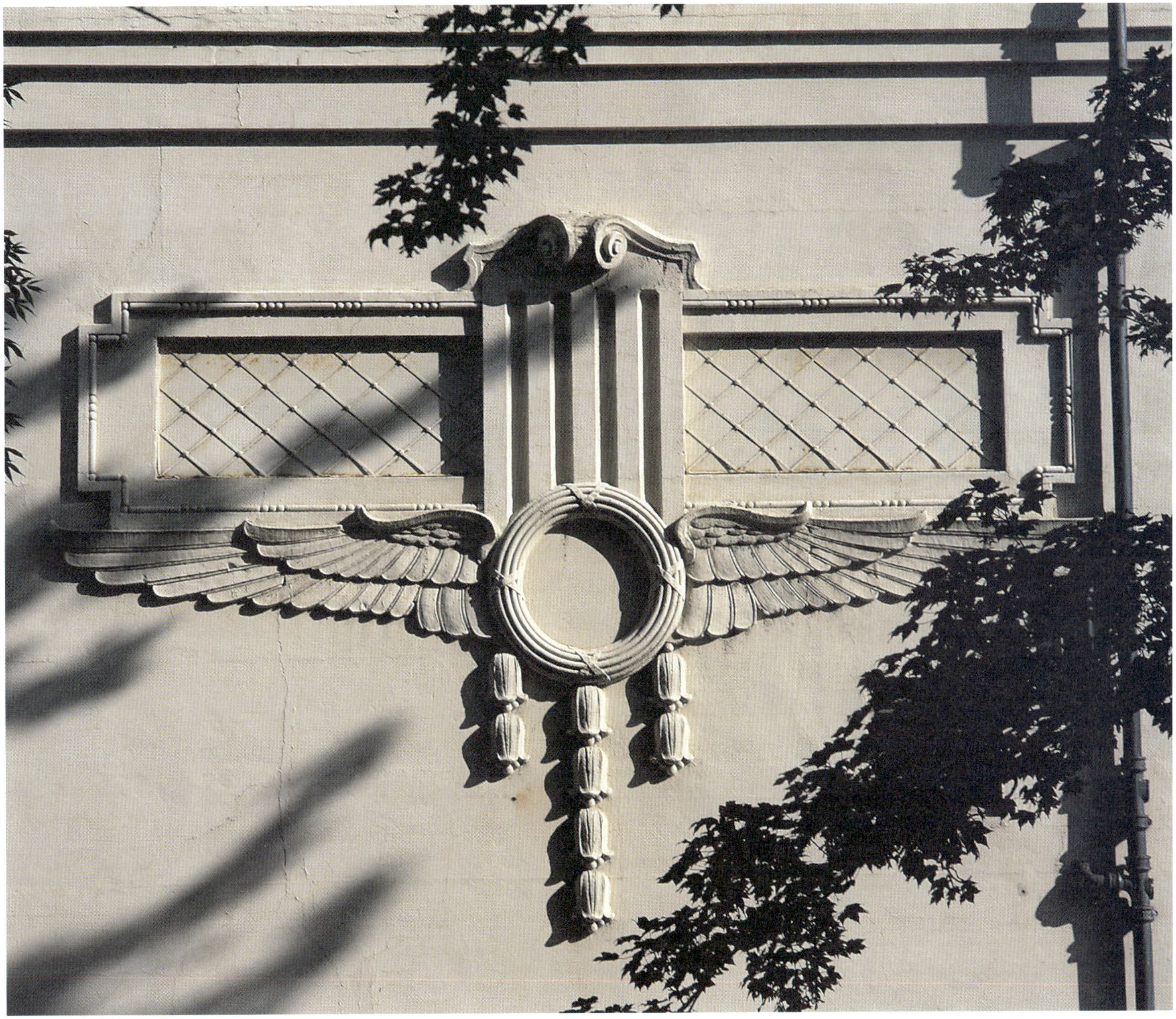

Goats and Gaudi in the Mina Valley

Watercress Road Allotments

A last relic of that lost nineteenth-century Bristol of collieries, foundries and working-class solidarity, these allotments in the Mina valley above Watercress Road and Boiling Wells Lane have a bedraggled and textured charm that neighbouring Eastville Park, heavily municipalised, cannot equal. Under the bean rows, ramshackle sheds and tilting greenhouses an old colliery adit still pours a powerful stream from its brick tunnel for a brief, headlong tumble alongside Church Path. This is a suburbia that has grown naturally child-friendly and hospitable to hen-pecked husbands – a place for hide-and-seek and blackberry picking, Tolkien country. That was what inspired Graham Caine and Martin Muller in 1986 to design their weirdly inventive 'gnome house' that writhes below the railway embankment, and the nearby café for the City Farm, in the same convoluted Art Nouveau. Part Antonio Gaudi, the Catalan architect, and part Roger Dean, the LP record-cover designer of the 1970s, these two buildings must have shaken the council planning department as they are both so shamelessly decorative. But they are also exactly right for the Mina valley, that suburban fantasy land where adults and children can still briefly escape from TV reality and video game pseudo-experience to get back in touch with the earth and the wild things.

Richard Church, one of the last Georgian poets, remembered how such strange landscapes can work:

> Lifting through the broken cloud there shot
> A searching beam of golden sunset-shine.
> It swept the town allotments, plot by plot,
> And all the digging clerks became divine -
> Stood up like heroes with their spades of brass,
> Turning the ore that made the realms of Spain!
> So shone they for a moment. Then, alas!
> The cloud-rift closed; and they were clerks again.

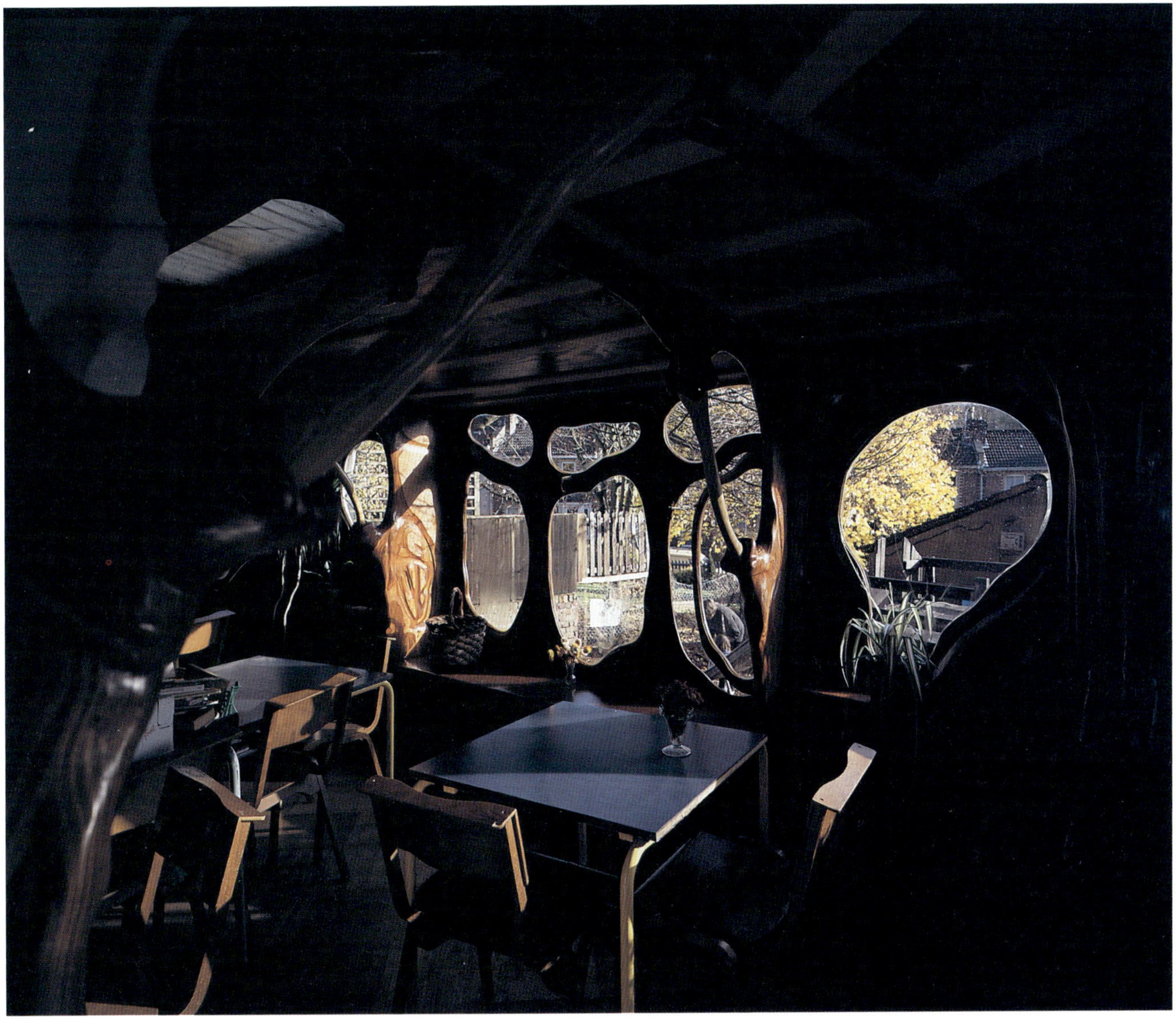

map 1

Netham Lock to Blaise Hamlet

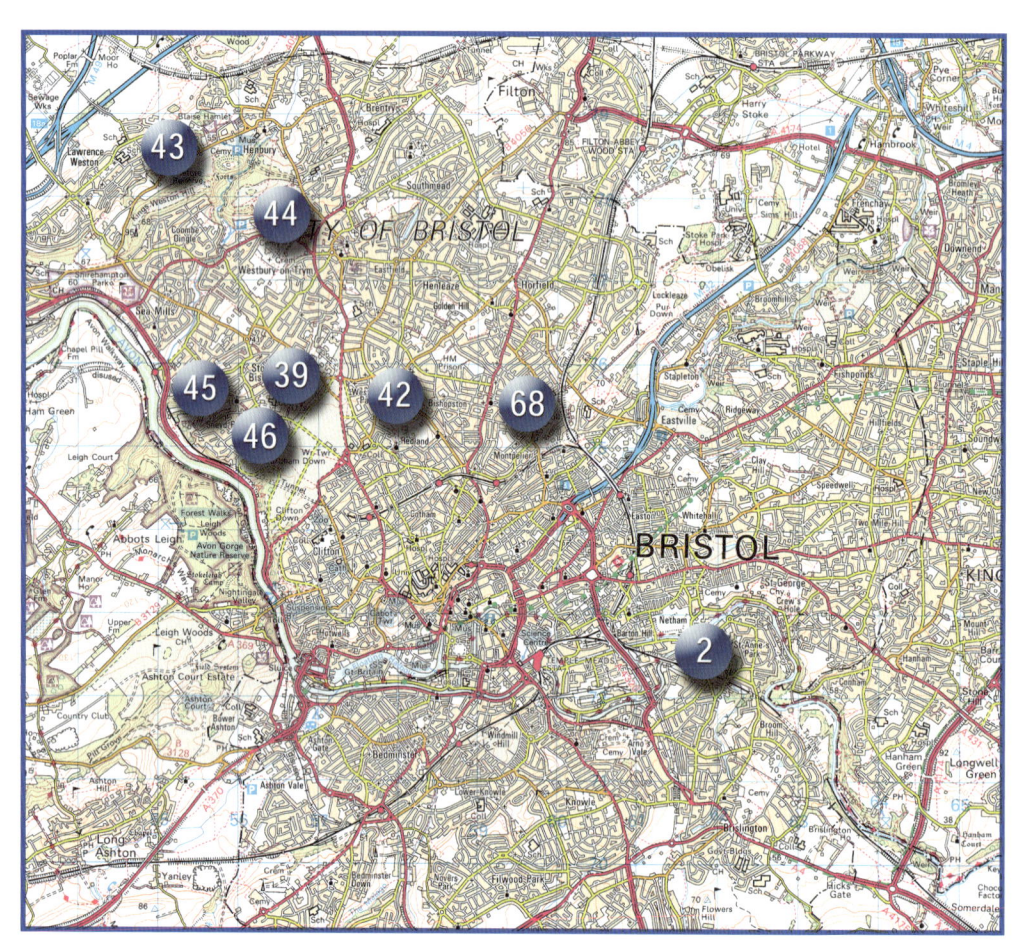

This map is reproduced from Ordnance Survey material with the permission of Ordnance Survey on behalf of Her Majesty's Office. ©Crown Copyright. MC031507.2000

map 2

The City

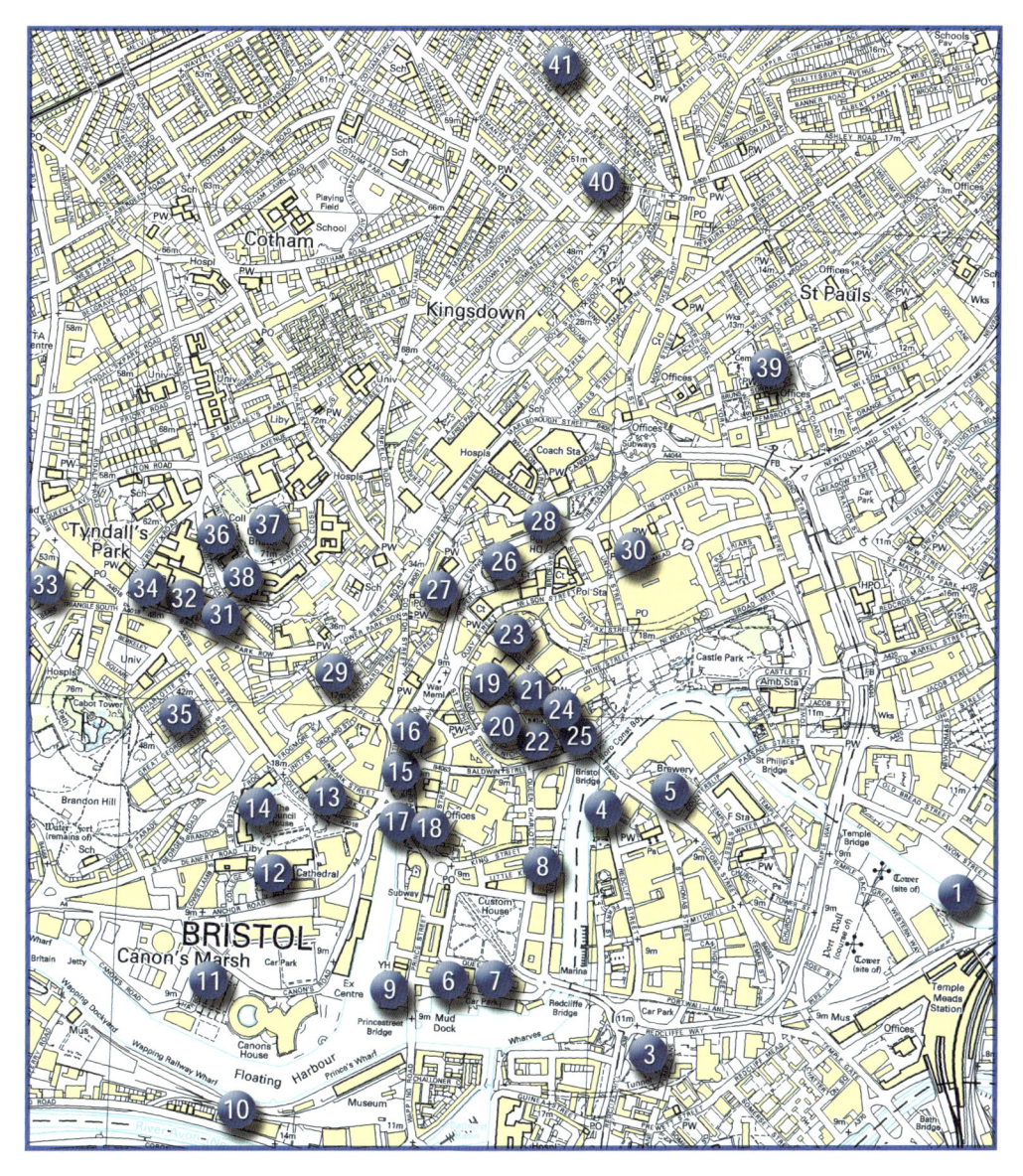

map 3

Clifton

index

01	AVON STREET BRIDGE		26	ELEVATED WALKWAYS, RUPERT STREET
02	NETHAM LOCK, FEEDER ROAD		27	HOTEL DU VIN, LEWIN'S MEAD
03	ST MARY REDCLIFFE, REDCLIFFE WAY		28	NO 1 BRIDEWELL, RUPERT STREET
04	ARMILLARY SPHERE, REDCLIFFE QUAY		29	THE RED LODGE, PARK ROW
05	8 VICTORIA STREET		30	WESLEY'S NEW ROOM, THE HORSEFAIR
06	THEKLA, THE GROVE		31	THE WILLS BUILDING, PARK ROW
07	RIVERSTATION, THE GROVE		32	BRISTOL MUSEUM AND ART GALLERY, QUEEN'S ROAD
08	THE GRANARY, WELSH BACK		33	PRO-CATHEDRAL, PARK PLACE
09	CABOT ON NARROW QUAY		34	BROWN'S, PARK ROW
10	THE STEAM CRANE, RAILWAY WHARF		35	ST GEORGE'S, GREAT GEORGE STREET
11	@ BRISTOL, CANONS ROAD		36	OLD BAPTIST COLLEGE, WOODLAND ROAD
12	BRISTOL CATHEDRAL, COLLEGE GREEN		37	THE ROYAL FORT, TYNDALL'S PARK
13	38 COLLEGE GREEN		38	THE CHEMISTRY BUILDING, CANTOCK'S CLOSE
14	THE COUNCIL HOUSE, COLLEGE GREEN		39	SURREY STREET AND DOWNLEAZE
15	FOUNTAINS AT ST AUGUSTINE'S PARADE		40	FREEMANTLE SQUARE, KINGSDOWN
16	NEPTUNE AT ST AUGUSTINE'S PARADE		41	41 GIBSON ROAD, COTHAM
17	SABRINA FOUNTAIN ON NARROW QUAY		42	REDLAND CHAPEL, REDLAND GREEN ROAD
18	BROAD QUAY HOUSE, NARROW QUAY		43	BLAISE HAMLET, HENBURY
19	LLOYDS BANK, CORN STREET		44	MERLIN CLOSE, WESTBURY-ON-TRYM
20	NAILS ON CORN STREET		45	PAINSWICK, OLD SNEED PARK
21	THE COUNCIL CHAMBER, CORN STREET		46	TOWERHIRST, CIRCULAR ROAD
22	ST NICHOLAS MARKET, CORN STREET		47	NAVIGATION LANTERN, AVON GORGE
23	THE EVERARD BUILDING, BROAD STREET		48	CUMBERLAND BASIN, CUMBERLAND BASIN ROAD
24	COLSTON IN ALL SAINTS, ALL SAINTS LANE		49	WINDSOR TERRACE, CLIFTON
25	HOGARTH'S TRYPTICH, ST NICHOLAS		50	CLIFTON SUSPENSION BRIDGE

index

51	PRINCE OF WALES CRESCENT, CLIFTON
52	FREELAND PLACE, CLIFTON
53	GRANBY HILL, CLIFTON
54	GOLDNEY RESIDENCES, GOLDNEY AVENUE
55	ST ANDREW'S WALK, CLIFTON
56	THE PARAGON, CLIFTON
57	113 PRINCESS VICTORIA STREET, CLIFTON
58	ST VINCENT'S PRIORY, SION HILL
59	AVON GORGE HOTEL, PRINCE'S LANE
60	SION HILL, CLIFTON
61	THE CAMERA OBSCURA, ST VINCENT'S ROCKS
62	CAMP HOUSE, CLIFTON DOWN
63	LITFIELD HOUSE, LITFIELD PLACE
64	BAUHAUS, LITFIELD ROAD
65	THE ZOOLOGICAL GARDENS, CLIFTON DOWN
66	THE RC CATHEDRAL, PEMBROKE ROAD
67	THE PICTURE HOUSE, WHITELADIES ROAD
68	THE ALLOTMENTS, WATERCRESS ROAD